There Once Was a Serpent

Serpent

A History of Theology in Limericks

First published by O Books, 2010
O Books is an imprint of John Hunt Publishing Ltd., The Bothy, Deershot Lodge, Park Lane, Ropley,
Hants, SO24 0BE, UK
office1@o-books.net
www.o-books.net

Distribution in:	South Africa
	Stephan Phillips (pty) Ltd
UK and Europe	Email: orders@stephanphillips.com
Orca Book Services Ltd	Tel: 27 21 4489839 Telefax: 27 21 4479879
tradeorders@orcabookservices.co.uk	
directorders@orcabookservices.co.uk	Text copyright Richard Kieckhefer 2009
Tel: 01235 465521 Fax: 01235 465555	
Int. code (44)	Design: Tom Davies
USA and Canada	ISBN: 978 1 84694 296 9
NBN	
custserv@nbnbooks.com	All rights reserved. Except for brief quotations
Tel: 1 800 462 6420 Fax: 1 800 338 4550	in critical articles or reviews, no part of this
	book may be reproduced in any manner without
Australia and New Zealand	prior written permission from the publishers.
Brumby Books	
sales@brumbybooks.com.au	The rights of Richard Kieckhefer as author have
Tel: 61 3 9761 5535 Fax: 61 3 9761 7095	been asserted in accordance with the
	Copyright, Designs and Patents Act 1988.
Far East (offices in Singapore, Thailand,	
Hong Kong, Taiwan)	
Pansing Distribution Pte Ltd	
kemal@pansing.com	A CIP catalogue record for this book is available
Tel: 65 6319 9939 Fax: 65 6462 5761	from the British Library.

Printed by Digital Book Print

O Books operates a distinctive and ethical publishing philosophy in
all areas of its business, from its global network of authors to
production and worldwide distribution.

There Once Was a Serpent

Serpent

A History of Theology in Limericks

Richard Kieckhefer

BOOKS

Winchester, UK
Washington, USA

Contents

There Once Was a Serpent

Introduction

There are people who read antiquarian book catalogues as avidly as they do books. Some years ago a friend of mine who couldn't get to sleep before spending time with these catalogues forwarded to me the notice of a very rare book he had seen in one, Bartholomew Lethaby's *Between God and the Devil: Truth and Deception in the History of Christian Theology*, published in a limited edition in 1914 by Spassvogel and Griesgram, a small London press that went out of business soon after the onset of the World War. I ordered the title and was pleasantly surprised to find I had not been preempted.

Six weeks or so later the book arrived in the mail, carefully wrapped by the book dealer, who operated in a remote village somewhere in Derbyshire, not far from the Peaks. The book itself was not disappointing. What I had not expected was the slender manuscript I found tucked into its pages by some previous owner, perhaps as a bookmark. On four sheets of unlined paper, written in a small and spiky hand, was a cycle of limericks dealing with the history of theology. Had it been sent me by mistake? Would it be possible to track the previous owner of the book, to see if he or she might wish the manuscript returned? I sealed it in an envelope and sent it to the book dealer, after making photocopies for myself.

Alas, the envelope reached England just after the bookseller had died, and there was no successor to help reunite the manuscript with its source. I contacted Lethaby's heirs, who compared the handwriting with his and determined that they were not alike, and in any case some of the limericks refer to theologians who wrote after Lethaby's death in 1927. I knew that F.S.C. Schiller wrote a history of philosophy in limericks, and it crossed my mind that he might have been the author of this cycle as well, but that conjecture was quickly dismissed: neither the style nor the approach to the subject matter was at all like Schiller's, and he too predeceased some of the theologians mentioned. In my scrupulosity I contacted friends in various parts of England and then even placed a short notice in *The Times*, thinking someone might speak up for the limericks or at least be able to identify their author. Nothing availed.

Up to this point I had merely glanced superficially through the limericks. Suspecting now that fate had meant me to have them, I began reading them more carefully, and before long I was engrossed in them. The more I studied the manuscript, the clearer it became that part of the cycle was missing. One of the limericks was missing its last two lines, while the next began with its short lines, with a substantial gap between in the chronology. Evidently the folded paper I had received was meant to have another leaf or two inserted in the fold. In a desperate attempt to find it, I flew to England from the United States and spent a week in a bed-and-breakfast near the antiquarian shop which by now was boarded-up. I made inquiries with anyone who might possibly know about the limericks.

Increasingly the project seemed futile, and I began to chafe at spending so much time in what seemed such a remote part of England. The sense of remoteness began to prey upon me.

One night I lay awake, quite sure I heard wolves howling outside the window of my bed-and-breakfast. Over breakfast the next morning the proprietor gently assured me there were in his experience no wolves in that part of Derbyshire.

Just when I was about to give up and head back across the Atlantic, however, I stopped for a dinner of fish and chips, and when I had finished my meal and was on the verge of throwing away the wrappings, I suddenly recognized some handwriting on the paper. To my amazement, the fish and chips had been wrapped in a sheet of unlined paper identical to the one that had been tucked into my book, but half as large, and it had written on it limericks and fragments that were missing from the cycle, slightly greasy but quite intact. My jubilation was tempered by the realization that there was still a missing sheet. Fortunately, however, within a week of my return home I found and purchased that on eBay.

Now that I had the entire cycle of limericks, my efforts focused on its content. The meaning of some verses was immediately clear, but I had to puzzle over others before I caught the drift or identified some key reference. I knew already what Gnostic syzygies and archons were, but it took time to find the relevance of "gourds and cucumbers." Holy Church Little was easy enough to identify as the notion of Marguerite Porete, and Pascal's wager was clear, but other allusions were more obscure. It became clear that the author of the limericks had relied at times on Lethaby's book; passages in Lethaby that were underlined provided clues for some of the more obscure verses.

By the time I had worked my way through the set, it occurred to me that others too might take some interest in this curious commentary on the history of Christian theology. And so it is that I present the limericks, with my own attempts to illuminate them, for whatever they may be worth. I give them in the order in which they occur in the manuscript, but their grouping into chapters is my own. Because the hand is clear and there was no need for emendations, it has not proven necessary to give editorial apparatus. All my effort has been to situate the limericks in the theological settings to which they belong.

Word somehow reached the fish-and-chip shop that I was planning to write a commentary on the limericks. As it happened, his brother-in-law was a lawyer, and when he heard about the project he planned to press legal charges, alleging that the sale of the fish and chips did not convey rights to the limericks on the wrapping.

While he was developing his case, however, the brother-in-law went on holiday and was eaten by a polar bear, and the vendor was unable to find another lawyer willing to take up the cause. I was thus spared litigation with a fish-and-chips seller over intellectual property rights, and the way was cleared for me to pursue my research and publication.

Chapter 1

Starting Out on One Foot or the Other: The Early Church

Several of the limericks in our anonymous collection seem fairly straightforward on a first reading, but then you go back, you read them again, and one line or another will leap out as puzzling. The very first limerick in the cycle might strike some readers as paradoxically both peculiarly obvious and yet obscure:

> Just one deity? That's not enough!
> We need syzygies, archons, and stuff!
> Give us gourds and cucumbers
> in unending numbers!
> An empty pleroma – that's tough!

The obvious part is the general context. Archons and syzygies are theological notions invoked by the Gnostics of late antiquity. An archon is a creator deity, distinct from the purely spiritual God who has nothing to do with material creation. A syzygy is a pair of divine aspects emanating from God, one male and one female. The pleroma is that great plenitude of beings – gods and countergods, archons and syzygies, and so forth, populating the spiritual world of the Gnostics. But gourds and cucumbers?

In much later centuries there was association in many people's minds between heretics and textile manufacture: weavers were famously suspect for an inclination toward heresy. But in the second and third centuries did the Gnostics draw many of their recruits from truck farmers and greengrocers?

No, what we have here comes from Irenaeus of Lyons, the

second-century bishop, theologian, martyr, and bane of the Gnostics. If limericks had been an option, Irenaeus might well have used them. He was in any case capable of wicked parody, and the first limerick in our cycle alludes to a parody that he wrote against his Gnostic opponents. He was lamenting their tendency to speculate about the origins of everything out of Oneness, Unity, and so forth. To say he was lamenting is no exaggeration: his text breaks out with "Woe! woe! Alas! alas!"

Irenaeus was sticking up for the simple Christian, the sort who in a later era would have held with calm assurance that Jesus read the King James Bible, and who certainly had no use for archons and syzygies and Onenesses. What irritates Irenaeus more than anything seems to be the sheer arbitrariness of the Gnostics' invention. How do they know that everything comes out of Oneness and these other principles? Where do they get the names for the principles they talk about? Basically, he says, they are making it all up. But anybody can play their game.

And just to show how it is done, Irenaeus invents his own Gnostic cosmology in which everything spills out of a power he calls First-Beginning, with which there coexists a power he calls a Gourd, and another that he calls Utter-Emptiness, and the Gourd and Utter-Emptiness, being one, bring forth "a fruit every-where visible, edible, and delicious, which in our language we call a Cucumber," and along with the Cucumber there is also a power he calls a Pumpkin, and then a great multitude of delicious pumpkins. He ends up with a cosmology of the pumpkin patch, just as good as any Gnostic cosmology.

In every religious tradition there are people who seek richness and multiplicity. They want to look at the divine light through a prism. They know that the light comes from a single source, but they prefer to see it refracted into the spectacle of all those colors that are, after all, contained within the original light. Other people are drawn instead to purity and parsimony. They insist on using a magnifying glass to bring the divine light into a single, clear point of burning intensity. The light comes in either case from the same source, but it gets either refracted or focused. Hindus use the prism. Muslims use the magnifying glass. Catholics use the prism, but perhaps not quite so much as Hindus. Protestants use the magnifying glass, not so insistently as orthodox Muslims. The Gnostics used the prism too, but with their own twist. They were less interested in seeing the glory of God refracted in the glories of the created world around them. The material world probably came, they thought, from some wicked counter-deity.

Phantasmagoric sunsets, the wonders of salvation history, and processions of saints held little attraction for the Gnostics. If divinity was to get refracted, it would have to be on the spiritual plane, and that is what held them spellbound.

Much of this the writer of the limericks could have gotten from Bartholomew Lethaby's book, which discusses the relationship between Irenaeus and the Gnostics (pp. 1-3). He (or she, except that the hand seems masculine) would also have read Lethaby's rather unusual theory that despite all his protestations Irenaeus was actually himself a crypto-Gnostic. He seems suspiciously good at parody; he must really have known how to do Gnostic-speak. Even after a great Gnostic library was discovered at Nag Hammadi, much of what we know of the Gnostics comes from Irenaeus. Was he perhaps doing his best to preserve the knowledge of Gnostic theories he cherished and was afraid might otherwise be lost? What better way than to catalogue them as errors.

Before long everyone was collecting heresies, and the orthodox opponents gave lasting notoriety to countless doctrines that would otherwise have passed into oblivion. But Lethaby suggests that Irenaeus's real insight was this: that if he could persuade other theologians to preoccupy themselves with argument against the Gnostics, if he could induce them to become truly obsessed with Gnostic error, sooner or later they would find ways of absorbing it into their own thinking. And it worked.

Before Irenaeus died (around AD 200), Clement of Alexandria was devising his own Christian Gnosticism, and his fellow Alexandrian Origen was soon exalting the value of a higher knowledge or *gnosis* within Christianity. All of which shows, according to Lethaby, that the best way to promote a doctrine is to attack it as vigorously as you can. And according to him, Irenaeus, one of the very earliest Christian theologians, had already learned this valuable lesson.

These Alexandrians and their heirs are famous not only for developing a more acceptably Christian version of Gnosticism but also for promoting allegorical interpretation of the Bible. The next limerick in the cycle might be called the theme song of the Alexandrian exegetes:

> The Bible reads better when seen
> through a rich allegorical screen.
> So a text that is vexed
> need not leave us perplexed:
> it can mean what we want it to mean.

Origen was in this way typical of the Alexandrian theologians. He found all sorts of problems in the Bible that could only be solved by interpreting it allegorically. How could there be morning and evening at creation even before the sun and moon and stars had been created? How can God have commanded the Israelites to massacre their enemies? Why would God have given Moses a list of kosher and forbidden foods that includes disgusting things nobody would think of eating in the first place? He gives an analogy that he claims to have gotten from a rabbi: the Bible is like a great mansion with many rooms, the bad news is that the door to each room is locked, the good news is that outside each door lies a key, the bad news is that in each case it is the wrong key, so the task is to discover which key opens which door. The scriptural exegete has to find the right key to open each passage of the Bible. Except that many passages can be opened by more than one key: a story can bear several meanings. The Song of Songs was an allegory for the love between Christ and the soul. But also for the love between Christ and the Church. And why not, as some soon claimed, also for the relationship between Christ and his mother Mary?

Alexandria was famous for this sort of exegesis. The theologians at Antioch tended rather to stick with the historical or "literal" meaning of the Bible. Alexandria versus Antioch was one of those great traditional rivalries, something like Eton versus Harrow, or Texas versus A&M, except that if there were footballs involved they were allegorical ones.

It wasn't only the Alexandrians who went in for allegorical reading. Saint Augustine, too, loved the idea of interpreting the Bible allegorically. Conundrums like the ones that bothered Origen nagged at him, too, and it was only when Saint Ambrose showed him how to allegorize that he realized the Bible could make sense. He allowed that in principle the Bible could mean both what one person sees and what another finds in it, and in fact God (the ultimate author of Scripture) was clever enough that He could pack an indefinite number of meanings into a single verse. The problem here is, in a sense, the same as the problem with Gnostic speculation: it seems capricious. The Bible means what you want it to mean. Lethaby was decidedly impatient with this approach to exegesis; he insisted that the Alexandrians and their heirs were making up their interpretations, and once you start making things up, he asked, where do you stop?

The question "where do you stop?" could and did lead to an answer that had far-reaching significance: Christianity came to its full authoritative development in the age of the Apostles, those who had lived with Christ, heard him preach, seen him perform miracles, taken flight to save their own skins when he was arrested, quivered in hiding until Pentecost, then burst forth on missionary journeys in all directions.

If you wanted to know what Christians believed and practiced, you consulted the Apostles. Or the Scriptures they and their closest associates wrote. Or their successors, the bishops, who sooner or later came to carry staffs because they were shepherds, but miters because they were like monarchs within their dioceses.

True Christianity was apostolic Christianity. And if the apostolic Scriptures weren't enough, and if the apostolic succession of the bishops wasn't enough to indicate who should interpret those scriptures, there was always the Apostles' Creed as a touchstone of doctrine. Legend has it that each of the twelve clauses in that creed was written by one of the apostles. Together, they sorted out sound, healthy doctrine from heresies. Did Marcion tell people that the creator of the Old Testament was an evil deity, different from the Father of Jesus? The Apostles' Creed said the Father made earth as well as heaven. Were there heretics who denied the resurrection of the body? The Apostles' Creed affirmed it.

In short, as our limerick writer tells us:

> The shepherds all met and agreed
> that their flock needed orthodox feed
> (not heretical swill!),
> so they sought to distill
> a healthy, digestible creed.

But the controversies continued, and by the early fourth century the key issue was exactly how the Son related to the Father. The Son was, to be sure, divine. But was he quite the same sort of divine being as the Father, or on a different level? Was he the first and most exalted of creatures? For the Arians, the Son was something like the Father but not quite. He was similar but not quite the same in substance: *homoiousios,* but not *homoousios.*

When the Council of Nicaea met to debate the matter in 325, its condemnation of the Arians was phrased partly in those terms. The iota remained out. The Son was *homoousios* with the Father, equal in divinity, according to the Nicene Creed.

> Is the Son consubstantial indeed
> with the Father? That's what's in the Creed.
> And with strictly set quotas
> on creedal iotas,
> the Arians cringe as they read.

Whose idea was this First Council of Nicaea, the first of all the ecumenical councils? No one bishop yet had the clout necessary to bring all the bishops together, but the emperor did have that clout, and the emperor happened to be the first Christian emperor, Constantine. Nominally Christian, perhaps, but that was enough. Christian at least in the sense that he cast his lot with the Christian Church, lavished favors upon it, brought churchmen into his court as advisers and orators, and expected in return that the Church would give his empire a solid ideological foundation. That meant that it had to be one more or less cohesive Church, and Constantine was not happy to have Arius and his Arian followers at odds with other Christians.

Legend tells us he had become Christian when he was about to go into battle and saw a vision of the cross of Christ glowing with light and bearing the inscription "In this sign you will conquer!" Now he had become Christian, and it was as though he had a nightmare in which one cross appeared bearing that slogan, and another alongside it saying "No, *this* cross!" and another with "Try this one!" Constantine was basically a soldier, not a theologian. As a soldier, he wanted order and discipline. Which is what he called the Council of Nicaea to ensure.

The teaching propounded by Arius
was for Constantine downright nefarious.
He said, "Let there be a
new creed of Nicaea,
lest heretics hector and harry us!"

Icons of the Council of Nicaea show the Arians trampled underfoot by the winners in the debate, the orthodox, while Constantine presides over the outcome. With this council the emperor had his nose under the theological tent, and for centuries there were emperors who took an interest in theology and Church affairs, and exerted what influence they could—which varied a great deal—in these areas.

Lethaby's prejudice on this point is characteristically unusual. He was enough of a believer in modern democracy to believe that warfare should be overseen by civilian authorities and not left to the generals, and he extended this principle to the realm of theology, believing it too important to be left to the theologians. Perhaps perversely, he carried these conclusions even further by suggesting the world would be a far better place if war were put in the hands of the theologians and theology were assigned to the generals. The theologians would debate the fine points of foreign affairs until long after the occasions for war had passed. And the generals would dismiss with indifference the hairsplitting subtleties that tend to detain the theologians. If Lethaby had a special fondness for Byzantine Christianity, it was because the generals who occupied the throne were among the most potent of the theologians—in his view.

Be that as it may, everyone but the Arians might have breathed a sigh of relief after 325, except that other issues arose, and each time there was a great sorting out in which heresy got distinguished from orthodoxy, like goats from sheep. While the Arian controversy centered on relations between the Father and the

Son, other quarrels had to do more with the divine and human natures within Christ.

Our limerick writer hints at one of the positions that got condemned as heresy:

> The One who does wonders, and glows
> far brighter than freshly bleached clothes –
> could he be the same
> as the one put to shame?
> Who ever would dare to suppose?

The Nestorians believed there were really two distinct persons, the divine Word and the human Jesus, who coexisted with each other more or less the way some good or evil spirit might enter into and possess a human being. The god Apollo might enter into and speak through the oracle at Delphi, yet Apollo and the oracle remained different. A demon might possess somebody, but the person didn't become a demon. The Word might enter into Jesus, even for his entire life, not just fleetingly, but still they were distinct persons. The Nestorians thus held there were two distinct persons with different natures, the divine Word and the human Jesus. The divine person performed miracles and glowed pure white on Mount Tabor. The human person suffered agony and death. But that made for problems, because if it was only a human person who was incarnate, crucified, and risen, how could he bring about human redemption? To redeem humanity, Christ had to assume humanity, body and soul, with all of its faculties. For the theologians who came to be recognized as orthodox, then, there was only a single person with two natures, divine and human.

One issue with profound implications for popular piety emerged in the course of the Nestorian controversy: what was the status of Christ's mother? For the Nestorians, she had borne the human Jesus but not the divine Logos. For the orthodox party, she gave birth to that single person, Jesus Christ, whose divine and human natures were already joined.

Thus, for the Council of Ephesus in 431, Mary was the Theotokos (or God-bearer).

> The mother gave birth, undefiled,
> not just to some plain human child
> but to God: so we read
> that the fathers decreed,
> while Diana just listened and smiled.

Diana here is the goddess, Diana of the Ephesians, Artemis to the Greeks, whose temple lay just outside Ephesus, down the road from the church where the Council of Ephesus was held.

Like Mary, Artemis/Diana combined virginity with fertility. The link is reinforced by the tradition that in her later life Mary settled in Ephesus. A long tradition of Christian appropriation is at work here, which writers such as C.S. Lewis have found entirely plausible: the myths of the pagans became fact in Christianity.

But other questions still needed to be resolved, and the Monophysites brought some of the most important to a head.

> Humanity adds nothing more
> than divinity already bore.
> For add what you will
> to infinity, still
> the sum is the same as before.

While the Nestorians held that Christ had two persons with two natures, the Monophysites claimed that he ultimately had only one person and nature, that being divine. He may have come down to earth and lain in a manger and all, but there was something unconvincing about all that, because all along he was really

God, and that made his humanity something of a pretense. The king might travel incognito among his people, but he never really became a commoner.

Or to use a mathematical analogy, God is infinite and cannot become finite. If you begin with a being who as God is infinite, and add humanity to that divinity, you have a being who remains infinite and hasn't really become finite.

In 451 the Council of Chalcedon split the difference by ruling that Christ had *two* natures joined in *one* person. Students like to speak of Christ as "part God and part man," something like a centaur of classical myth. That might be marginally easier to imagine, but it's not what the Council of Chalcedon had in mind. It insisted that Christ was *fully and truly* divine, and *fully and truly* human, not half and half. In this as in many cases, dogma insists on having it both ways, leaving it to the theologians to puzzle out how the two options can be reconciled, and perhaps also to the poets, who may have more chance of success.

The next limerick moves off in a rather different direction, introducing rather different issues, and either you get it or you don't. In any event, it leads us quickly to another of the fascinating ways theology can lead to charges of heresy.

"Peer pressure is always a threat,
and I can't give up lust, not just yet!
So give your command
– but give also your hand,
and *you* meet the challenge you've set."

Fortunately, Lethaby has an entire chapter on Saint Augustine of Hippo, which helps to make sense of this and the next few limericks. The first clue here is the use of quotation marks. Augustine's *Confessions* constitute one long prayer, addressed to God, reviewing the story of Augustine's complicated life and praising God for his aid. (The Latin *Confessiones* means here, in the first instance, "praises".)

Augustine judged his own failings severely. He tells a famous story about how as a boy he stole pears one day and then threw them to the pigs. Why did he do it? Was he attracted to evil for its own sake? That would be demonic; those of us who are not quite demons do evil because we are tricked into seeing it as good. Part of the reason Augustine stole the pears is that he was traveling with a band of young hooligans, and they will do just about anything under peer pressure. The attraction of pears turns out to be largely the goading of peers.

Before long Augustine got into worse trouble, when puberty brought him to habits that were hard not only to resist but to *want* to resist. His will was divided, as it so often is. He prayed, famously, "Give me continence and chastity – but not quite yet!"

But the theological crux comes not with this but in the last three lines of the limerick. In one of the later chapters of the *Confessions*, Augustine says to God, "Give what you command, and command what you will." In fact, he says this fully five times, just to make sure God gets the point.

A pious British monk named Pelagius also got the point. Augustine was telling God that he could command anything, even chastity, but Augustine was too weak-willed to meet God's challenge, so he asked God to do it for him, or to give him the grace that would make it possible. Pelagius (and succeeding generations of Pelagians) thought this was nonsense: we all have as much strength of will as Adam had at his creation, and we only need to buck up and use the moral strength we were born with.

The debate between Augustine and Pelagius lasted years; in some circles it is still going on. The consequences for theology have been huge.

Some are damned and foredoomed as depraved,
while a few are predestined and saved.
Though we can't tell just who,
it has nothing to do
with how righteously we have behaved.

Augustine began with the simple but firm conviction that we depend on God for everything, and he ended by drawing the conclusion that God predestines us for salvation, or not. Because of the original sin we inherit from Adam, we are all born sinners. We love ourselves rather than God. Even if we try to become lovers of God, that quest is motivated by self-love, and we remain sinful lovers of self. The only way we can be plucked from this mire is by grace, and if God gives that grace it is because he means for us to be saved, and so we will be. Only a fixed number of people are among the chosen. The rest are left to their inevitable fate of damnation. Does God choose those he knows in advance will respond well to his offer of grace? No, God's choice is made without regard for how we have acted, will act, or might act. Is this fair? To us it seems not, but we creatures cannot challenge God's judgment.

Thus the doctrine of predestination, which Augustine takes as grounded in Saint Paul's epistles, and which succeeding generations in Western Christianity found worked out in Augustine. Martin Luther and John Calvin believed in predestination, but then so did Thomas Aquinas. Lethaby points out this difference: that for Augustine predestination begins in reflection on the soul and its weakness, and serves primarily as a statement about the soul, while for Thomas it is sandwiched between questions about the power and the providence of God, and is thus chiefly a statement about God. Still, whatever the permutations of context, the influence of Augustine in the West has been pervasive.

That influence went well beyond the doctrine of predestination. In other areas of theology, too, Augustine is a towering figure, as our limerick writer seems to have known:

"So you think that you might understand
how three can be one – that's just grand!
While you work on that notion
I'll empty the ocean
right into this hole in the sand!"

For this the inspiration does not come from Lethaby, but the legend is well enough known. It evidently goes back to the thirteenth century, when the Cistercian monk Caesarius of Heisterbach told it about an anonymous schoolman, and the Dominican friar Thomas of Cantimpré turned it into a story about Augustine. The story has it that the saint was walking back and forth on the seaside one day, trying to make theological sense of the Trinity. How could there be three persons – Father, Son, and Holy Spirit – in one God? Not three Gods, or three aspects of God, or three parts of God, but three persons in just a single God?

The mystery didn't seem open to logical resolution, but Augustine paced back and forth on the sand trying to puzzle it out. Then he saw a small child playing in the sand, and he asked the child what he was doing. The boy said he was trying to empty the water from the sea into the hole he had dug on the beach. Augustine said, "You can't do that – that's impossible!" And the child, who was clearly no ordinary child, but an angel in some versions, Christ himself in others, said, "It's no less impossible for you to understand the Trinity."

One might have thought the inventor of the legend would make it three children who speak with a single voice, but that's not the way the legend goes.

But is the legend, in any case, fair to Augustine? His heroically long writing *On the Trinity* begins by establishing from the Bible that God is triune: that there is one God, but three persons. His evidence comes largely from the Old Testament, which might seem to some readers perverse, something like turning to Adam Smith's *Wealth of Nations* to find a justification for progressive taxation. (It is, in fact, there.)

Then, having established from the Bible that God is triune, Augustine poses the question what this could possibly *mean*. At this point he seeks analogies to help give an intellectual handle. Since there were no shamrocks where he came from, he had to find other analogies for the Trinity. After he has ruled out one analogy after another, he settles on the psychological one: the persons of the Trinity are something like the major faculties in the human soul. The root faculty of memory corresponds to the Father, while understanding corresponds to the Son, and will to the Holy Spirit. He knows the analogy is flawed, but it is the best he can do, and surely among the best anyone has proposed. In any case, he isn't trying to *prove* that God is triune. That much he has established from revelation in Scripture, in which he has faith. And he lays down the key axiom that if he did not first have that faith, he would never have understanding. He has to accept the concept before he can begin to puzzle out what it might mean.

Augustine took a great deal from Plotinus, the pagan philosopher and fountainhead of Neoplatonic philosophy. In fact, he said in his *Confessions* that when he read Plotinus he found there all the major teachings of Christianity except the incarnation. The influence is perhaps nowhere clearer than in Augustine's understanding of evil. He fretted a great deal about evil. In the *Confessions*, he asked where moral evil came from in his own experience. Later, in *The City of God*, when Rome had been sacked by the barbarians, he grappled with the problem of evil in the broader context of human affairs. His answer, which came by and large from his reading of the pagan Neoplatonist philosopher Plotinus, has satisfied some but not all readers.

In God's providential creation
there seems to be much tribulation,
but the evils we're fleeing
have no real being:
they're nothing at all – mere privation.

The analogy of heat and cold seems apt: heat is a form of energy, and cold is not a different energy but a lack of heat. That is not to say that frigid winds have no power to chill the bone and bring misery, even death. It is only to say that they do so by depriving the body of the warmth it needs. Evil is privation of the good. Hatred is a lack of charity. Despair is a lack of hope. Disbelief is a lack of faith. Human fallenness is a lack of that proper ordering of soul and body that humans are meant to have. Is disease a lack of health? Yes, even if we recognize that there are disease agents, these are not in themselves evil, but the disruption to proper bodily function is another type of privation.

Here the enemies were the Manichaeans, who believed in goodness and evil as rival principles in the universe. For Augustine there was only one ultimate principle, that of goodness, even though he looked all around himself, and within himself, and saw evil everywhere. All of creation groaned under the weight of its disorder, its lack of the goodness it was meant to enjoy. And yet goodness would *ultimately* prevail, and even the evils might contribute toward some ultimate goodness, much as in a work of art the balance of light and dark contributes toward a greater whole. This is neither pure optimism nor pure pessimism, but theological optimism tempered by experiential pessimism.

Lethaby raises an interesting comparison here. Because Augustine believed in a universe grounded in goodness, he had to explain evil as a privation of the good. The nineteenth-century philosopher Schopenhauer believed in a universe grounded in evil: in a blind, destructive, and ultimately self-destructive Will.

For him, then, the problem was how to explain instances of goodness, and his answer, nicely mirroring Augustine's, was fundamentally that goodness is the absence of evil. Put simply, moral goodness is the suspension of the evil one normally expects, the compassionate restraint from harm. Aesthetic goodness consists in a contemplative release from willing. And the ultimate goodness for Schopenhauer is personal annihilation, his version of nirvana, a privation of existence itself. In short, goodness and not evil is privative. One only wonders how Lethaby came to know Schopenhauer.

Apart from Augustine, another major channel through which Neoplatonism flowed into Christian theology was Dionysius the Areopagite, or rather the Syriac monk of the late fifth and early sixth century who represented himself by that name. This Dionysius, in his book *On the Divine Names*, worked out a schema of circular, linear, and spiral motion that applied, but differently, to angels, to souls, and to God.

> At rest, in a circle suspended,
> or tracing a line, and extended,
> the angel heeds both
> blessed stillness and growth:
> the spiral shows how these are blended.

The angels (or "divine intelligences") move in a circle when they are absorbed in the light that streams out of the divine Source, the Beautiful and Good. But they are also sent out to creatures, offering them guidance in a world of growth and decay, and when they do that they move in a line. It is when they combine the two, tending to creatures while still turning around the divine Source, that they move in a spiral pattern. For the soul, the three types of motion are all ways of knowing God: by turning within themselves (circular), by attending to external realities and being uplifted from their multiplicity to the simplicity of contemplation (linear), and by discursive reasoning (spiral). And these movements can be seen in God too: in his steadfast sameness (circular), in the procession of all things outward from him (linear), and in the simultaneity of the procession and his fecund stillness (spiral).

When Dionysius wrote in this mode, he was making affirmations about God. But ultimately the affirmative gave way to the negative way, to the realization that all human perceptions, conceptions, and language are inadequate to the divine.

> Neither body, nor spirit, nor mind,
> or anything else of that kind,
> neither living or dead
> can be properly said
> of the Cause that cannot be defined.

This is the culmination of Dionysius's *Mystical Theology*. He has shown how the mystic can rise from purgation, through illumination, into union with God. But what can the soul united with God ever say about the divine Cause of all things? Nothing. Even to say that this Cause is being or goodness or life is to falsify the ineffable reality of the divine.

Yet another theologian profoundly influenced by pagan philosophical traditions was the sixth-century writer Boethius, who in his *Consolation of Philosophy* sounds indeed rather more like a pagan than a Christian. Boethius had fallen into disfavor with Theodoric, the Arian king ruling in Italy, and he was sitting on death row. Lady Philosophy came to him in a vision, with the unenviable task of persuading him that his situation was not so bad as it seemed.

How happy we'd be if the love
that rules in the heavens above
could rule in our hearts,
as balm for the darts
that we suffer when Fate comes to shove.

Lady Philosophy had clearly read her Plato and her Stoics. She may also have read the Bible, but she shows less evidence of that, and in any case she did not come to persuade Boethius that he should accept Jesus as his personal savior. One poetic passage in the *Consolation* is a soaring exaltation of the love that governs the heavens. How blessed human life would be, she exclaims, if it too were governed by that same love! Later she teaches Boethius about the relationship between Providence and Fate. They are part of the same process, actually, but Providence represents the perspective of the divine mind that orders all things, while Fate is what mortals here below perceive in the empirical world as they are tossed about on the billowing waves of adversity. The trick is to learn that Fate is actually the working-out of Providence, that the loving God can draw good out of evil, and that things are thus better than they seem, even if you are about to be beheaded.

When Augustine and Boethius were both long dead, they shared one twist of Fate that neither would have anticipated: the same church in Pavia claims the bones of both.

Already in the earliest generations of Christianity, theology went hand-in-hand with morality, and this remained the case when monasticism, a movement centrally concerned with leading the good and holy life, arose in the fourth and fifth centuries.

The monks of late antiquity had much to say about demons, temptations, and sin. The fourth-century monk Evagrius Ponticus was among the first to undertake a categorization of sins. His list included greed, fornication, avarice, sadness, anger, accidia, vainglory, and pride. With editorial help from Gregory the Great in the sixth century, it evolved into the classical Seven Deadly Sins: pride, covetousness, lust, anger, gluttony, envy, and sloth.

Our limerick writer gives the list, although not in the classical order:

> Gluttony, greed, and desire,
> with pride, sloth, envy, and ire
> – that miserable medley
> of sins that are deadly –
> will bring us to brimstone and fire.

The opposite list is known as the contrary virtues: chastity, temperance, charity, and so forth. But vices have always had better press than virtues, and the Seven Deadly Sins have always been better known than their opposites, if not better loved.

Many people think of Augustine as a stern, uncompromising moral rigorist. Actually he was less so than many of his contemporaries. The Pelagians, who thought people should pick themselves up by their own moral bootstraps, were less tolerant of human frailty than Augustine. And his elder contemporary Jerome had if anything a more broodingly negative view of sexuality:

> How shameful, so lewdly to wallow
> in pleasures and passions so hollow!
> But virginity grieved
> means more virgins conceived:
> *elicitur bonum ex malo.*

Jerome was a monk, and he would gladly have seen everyone else become monks and nuns. He may have been tormented by unspeakably powerful sexual temptations, which he met by

24

pummeling his body into submission to principle. Married life was not for him. Could others find sanctity in it? The best he could see was that marriage would result in offspring who themselves would begin their days as virgins, and might be persuaded to end them the same way. And thus, as in other ways, God could draw good out of evil.

But for exuberant sternness, the prize goes to Tertullian, the late second-century lawyer turned early third-century theologian, who condemned the wearing of finery and attendance at any public entertainment, not just circuses and gladiatorial contests but even plays and sporting events. He tells a story of a woman who went to a theater and got possessed by a demon. The demon, called to accounts, insisted he was within his rights because the woman had entered his domain. The one form of public entertainment Tertullian did approve was the grand spectacle that the righteous will enjoy at the Last Judgment.

> What a spectacle then we'll behold,
> when the sinners' fierce torments unfold
> one by one. What a treat!
> So reserve a good seat,
> before the best tickets are sold.

This is actually not a parody. The original, Tertullian's *On the Spectacles*, is far stronger. He talks about the sinful actors impressively lamenting their tragic roles, the comic actors twisting amusingly in the fire, the athletes tossed about in the flames, and he asks which of these sights will most excite his wonder and arouse his laughter. This is not mere sternness, but sadism. Tertullian eventually gave up on mainstream Christianity and joined the Montanists, a sect that sought greater purity in their isolation as they waited for the heavenly Jerusalem to descend and give a fitting abode for the morally fit but few.

Throughout the early centuries of Christianity, if you belonged to the Latin-speaking Church of the West, or the Greek- or Syriac- or other-speaking Churches of the East, you ultimately belonged just to the Church, unless you happened to be an Arian or a Monophysite or a member of some other group that had been branded as heresy. Christianity was not broken up geographically, as it later came to be. But eventually Latins and Greeks became estranged over various issues, one of them being the famous *filioque* controversy:

> That the Spirit proceeds from the Son
> as well as the Father is one
> of those pestilent isms
> that lead us to schisms.
> One word, and all dogma's undone!

The Nicene Creed and its later revision at the First Council of Constantinople made a subtle distinction: the Son is *begotten* of the Father, while the Holy Spirit *proceeds* from the Father. The Western Church, beginning in the sixth century, decided that the Holy Spirit proceeds not just from the Father but also from the Son. Thus, the classic Latin version of the Creed, set to music by all the great liturgical composers of Western Christendom, proclaims that the Spirit proceeds *ex patre filioque*, "from the Father and the Son", and that one word *filioque* has left Orthodox Christians quivering ever since. The West was inspired in part by Augustine's suggestion that the Spirit is the bond of love between the Father and the Son.

By the ninth century, Patriarch Photius of Constantinople was railing against the interpolation of the *filioque* as a heresy. The Eastern, or Orthodox, world has argued that it relegates the Spirit to a subordinate position within the Trinity. There are Orthodox Christians who see this as the fountainhead of all Western errors.

Bartholomew Lethaby floated the rather dubious hypothesis

that the controversy began because the Greeks did not understand Latin grammar, they construed *Filioque* as a proper name, and they wondered who this "Father Filioque" was from whom the Latins thought the Spirit proceeded. Once the error was pointed out to them, Lethaby imagines, it no longer mattered. They had made up their minds that the Latins were wrong. And once a quarrel is started, even if it rests on a simple misunderstanding, it takes on a life of its own, and both sides find further and perhaps deeper reasons to continue disagreeing.

On this last point, if on nothing else, Lethaby was surely right.

Chapter 2

Theology Goes to School: The Middle Ages

The early Middle Ages, from the fall of the Roman Empire up to the turn of the millennium, used to be called the Dark Ages, the age of the barbarians. Socially and politically there was indeed quite a bit of disorder, but then this is the age that gave us something that remains important: Europe. The old Mediterranean world of antiquity was replaced by a new world of European culture that extended from Ireland to Hungary and from Italy to Scandinavia.

Classical learning survived more widely than had previously been thought, largely because of the monks. They knew their Augustine, and some of them knew about Dionysius, but they were mainly absorbed in reading the Bible, praying the Bible, meditating on the Bible and interpreting the Bible. For most monks of the age, it was a commonplace that the Bible has multiple levels of meaning, and our limerick writer takes note of that assumption:

> The literal sense is the story,
> while for teaching we seek allegory.
> The moral tells when
> we've been naughty – but then
> anagogy prefigures our glory.

There was some dispute about exactly how many meanings a verse in the Bible might have, but one widespread viewpoint was enshrined in the idea of fourfold interpretation. Jesus went into the Temple and drove out the money-changers. That's the literal level, the biblical narrative, taken as straightforward historical fact. But if we want to find some instruction about Christ and his place in salvation within the narrative, we go further and seek the allegorical meaning: Christ's driving the money-changers out of the Temple is an allegory for his driving out the entire system of Jewish sacrificial ritual. If we want ethical reflection, we look for the moral meaning: Christ enters into the soul and purges it of evil. And if we want to know about our fate in eternity, we ask about the anagogical meaning: Christ enters into the heavens and drives the demonic hosts (the "princes of the air") out of them.

Bartholomew Lethaby thought that a new and distinctively medieval theology erupted on the scene in the late eleventh century with Anselm of Canterbury and his ontological argument for the existence of God. Of course Lethaby was writing in the early twentieth century, and everything has become more complicated since then, even the history of medieval theology. Anselm was not writing in a vacuum; he had his own predecessors and teachers. Still, Anselm and his ontological argument make as good a starting-point as any for this part of the limerick cycle that is so indebted to Lethaby.

> A being than which there is nought
> to be sought that could even be thought
> to be greater – must be!
> Everyone must agree,
> and if some fool doesn't, he ought!

The ontological argument comes out of Anselm's desire to find a single clinching argument for God's existence. He had earlier given a series of arguments, but this one was his theological pièce de resistance. Some might wonder why in the late eleventh century it was necessary to prove God's existence. Was anyone doubting it? The Jews and Muslims believed it. The heretics believed it. If you wanted to find a professed atheist, you had to go to the Psalms, where it is the fool who says in his heart, "There is no God!" (Psalm 14:1, 53:1). So Anselm's adversary is the Psalmist's fool. Of course even the fool knows what the term "God" means: a being so great that you can't even think of a greater. What would such a being be like? A being a greater than which cannot be conceived would have to have total knowledge, total power, total goodness, total beauty. But – says the fool – one thing this being does not have is existence. Aha! says Anselm – the fool has just contradicted himself. Because he has spun out this equation:

A: God
= B: a being a greater than which cannot be conceived
= C: a being with all knowledge, power, goodness, etc., but not existence

And Anselm points out that it is possible to imagine an even greater being, one who has total knowledge, power, goodness, beauty, *and existence*. So A equals B, but B does not equal C. When the fool denies existence to God, he is indulging in a self-contradiction. God has to exist, by definition. Q.E.D.

This ontological argument is a ball that has gone back and forth across the net many times. René Descartes and Gottfried Leibniz and Karl Barth and many others have believed in it, in one form or other. Thomas Aquinas and Immanuel Kant and others have argued against it. One objection says, basically, that existence doesn't really belong in a definition. When you define a table, you say it's an item of furniture with a flat top and supporting legs, but you don't have to add to your definition that tables really exist. A dictionary that put existential tags on all its definitions (Grommets exist, Hoopoes exist, Yetis may or may not exist) would be needlessly cluttered. Even if you are defining a unicorn, is it enough to say it is a horse with a single horn growing out of its forehead? Calling it legendary is extra information that arguably is or isn't really needed in the definition. So the fool was within bounds in defining God as he did but then, after giving his definition, shrugging his shoulders and calling God a figment.

Anselm actually took something like this objection into account and had a reply. The objection might work, except that with God what we are talking about is not just existence but *necessary* or non-contingent existence. And it does belong to the definition of God that, while other beings depend on him, he depends on nothing else. Creatures have conditional being; God has necessary being. The fool remains unconvinced, of course. And Anselm is not surprised, because that's what you would expect of a fool.

It may have been only a minority of readers who accepted Anselm's ontological argument, but on another matter his way of viewing things became so widely accepted that for centuries it was taken for granted in the Western Church. It has to do with atonement for sin and with the incarnation of Christ.

> The debt fell to mankind alone,
> but only our God could atone,
> so a God-man was needed.
> The point, all conceded,
> *et Christo remoto*, was shown.

The key here is in the Latin bit. Even setting Christ aside, *Christo remoto*, Christ had to do the work of atonement. In other words, one can show even without scriptural revelation that it was necessary for the God-man to atone for human sin. What were the alternatives? God might have left all humankind to damnation, but not without frustrating his own purposes, and that would not do. He might have just pardoned humankind without any punishment, but that would have meant letting mercy cancel out justice, and that would not do. He could have let humankind (or perhaps some angel) make up for the offense to his honor, but creatures already owe God all honor and obedience, and nothing they render will undo the damage, so again that will just not do. The only possibility left is that God's own Son, who was without sin and thus not required to die, should enter into human flesh. Having become thus incarnate, he could die in an act of free, supererogatory obedience. As human, Christ could bear the burden and pay the price that humanity *needed* to pay. As God, he was *able* to pay that price.

Earlier theologians had privileged other ways of talking about atonement. It was a combat between Life and Death: Christ as the prince of life triumphed over Satan the prince of death. Or it was a bit of trickery: Christ tricked Satan into claiming the Sinless One in death, thus breaking the rules and forfeiting all his claims over humankind. Or it was simply a redemption in the original sense of that term, a buying back. All of these perspectives can be seen hinted at somewhere in the Bible, but Anselm's notion of "substitutionary atonement" is one that is less explicitly there than others. After Anselm this became the primary theology of atonement.

The limerick points out that Anselm was trying to establish the necessity of the incarnation even setting biblical revelation aside, even *Christo remoto*. Here and in his ontological argument, Anselm was trying to find clinching arguments that would persuade the unbeliever. Yet he insisted, in apparent self-contradiction, that theology begins with faith and proceeds to rational grasp of what is believed. Theology is faith seeking understanding, *fides quaerens intellectum*. So which is it: does theology set out to find clinching arguments that can lead the unbeliever to belief, or does it presuppose belief and move toward understanding? The simple answer is that Anselm is showing the consonance of reason and revelation. It may be that we in fact begin with firm and unshakeable faith, and that we will not lose that faith if reason turns up empty-handed. But he trusts that it will not, because he trusts that reason and revelation will lead to the same conclusions, and in this he does anticipate the Scholastics who came after him.

Medieval writers were very fond of the Psalm verses "Mercy and truth have met together, justice and peace have kissed" (Psalm 85:10), and they represented Mercy, Truth, Justice, and Peace as the four "Daughters of God," who debated before the divine throne about what should be done with humankind. Mercy and Peace pleaded for leniency. Justice and Truth insisted that letting humankind off without proper punishment was not fitting. The solution – incarnation and atonement by the God-man Christ – satisfied everyone.

> Stern Justice cries, "Doom to that race!"
> while Mercy pleads, "Grant them some grace!"
> Truth urges, "Be firm!"
> and so Peace starts to squirm,
> but Christ says, "I'll die in their place."

Lethaby in a rare whimsical moment pondered whether Anselm had exhausted all the possibilities in his argument by elimination: could God not have spared his Son and sent one of his Daughters? Considering how scrupulous Anselm was to rule out all the alternatives, it is a bit surprising that this option did not occur to him. In any event, Anselm's chief goal was to show how revelation and reason could embrace, how the Bible and philosophy could meet on friendly terms.

Later in his life, Anselm became an archbishop of Canterbury. For centuries, monks who had proven themselves good administrators had gotten tapped for work outside the monastery, in the Church and even in secular government. Gregory the Great was the first monk to become a pope, in the late sixth century. For the rest of his life he lamented the loss of contemplative peace and quiet. But monks who were called on for service realized they were needed. They would have preferred the contemplative life to the active life, but they settled for the "mixed life" in which they mingled prayer with service.

> Contemplation will always entice,
> yet the world keeps us caught in its vise.
> A deep, mystical kiss
> would surely be bliss –
> but a peck on the cheek may suffice.

Alongside the monastic schools, the twelfth century saw the blossoming of the so-called cathedral schools, forerunners of the universities: places where non-monks could go for study. For historians, the cathedral schools are an important element in "the renaissance of the twelfth century." For contemporaries, they could be sites of increasingly bitter controversy. And one of the most famous and infamous theologians of the era, Peter Abelard, thrived on controversy – at least on provoking it, if not on grappling with the attacks on him that ensued.

> "My purpose is not to confuse,
> as my doltish opponents accuse,
> but to make better known
> that each *sic* has its *non*:
> Truth is one – but truths travel in twos."

Sic et non, or *Yes and No*, was the title of a compilation by Abelard. The work raises a series of 158 theological issues, some of which might never have occurred to the reader without Abelard's prodding: Is God the cause even of evils? Did Christ or the saints wish to die? Did all the apostles except John have wives? For each question he gave a digest of opinions by early Christian writers, some tending toward one answer, others toward the opposite. He said his purpose was to help fledgling theologians think for themselves, which he thought of as a good thing for them to do. Was it? Some of his contemporaries said yes, other no.

The notion of bringing together multiple authorities on a theological issue is one that Peter Lombard built upon in his *Sentences*, which became the standard starting-point in theology: one cut one's teeth as a theologian by writing a commentary on the *Sentences*. But Peter Lombard was less of a smart aleck than Abelard, and his purpose was not to throw up a dust storm of conflicting opinions, but to survey the accepted authorities with an eye toward consensus. Our limerick writer shows no interest in him.

In any case, it was not so much *Sic et Non* that got Abelard into trouble but rather his teachings on the Trinity. For these he was condemned by more than one council. As one of the most accomplished religious poets of his day, he wrote numerous concluding doxologies, praising the Trinity in eloquent and creative ways. But it was his dense theological prose that got him into trouble for representing the Father as power, the Son as wisdom, and the Holy Spirit as goodness, in a way that led readers like Bernard of Clairvaux to see modalism: the view that the three persons are not truly distinct, but merely aspects or modes of God.

> *Me* a heretic? Say it's not so!
> In a life of misfortune and woe,
> first my body gets clipped,
> then my teaching gets ripped
> by that miserable monk from Clairvaux!"

Abelard laments his theological condemnations in his autobiographical *History of Calamities*. But it was not only these condemnations that made his life a chain of calamities. It was also the notorious affair with his pupil Heloise that ended abruptly when her relatives seized him and castrated him.

Bernard of Clairvaux himself was one of those figures who loom large on every stage. He made a profound impact when he preached the Second Crusade and promoted the Knights Templars. He was famous for antiheretical outbursts, directed not only at Abelard. He preached against the Cathars, and when they claimed they traveled together, men and women, without having sex, he scoffed that this was harder than raising the dead, and he *knew* they couldn't do that. His early biographers portray him as a model of passionate austerity, a man whose fasting left him a physical wreck, yet he kept on going. He could pray daily in the monastery church and take no notice of its design, being oblivious to his merely physical environment. He insisted it was only in the famously rigorous Cistercian order that he could work out his salvation, and he told others that if they did not follow him inside the monastery walls they were in danger of eternal perdition. The order became prominent in large part because of his promotion. He was also a mystic, passionate about the living experience of a living God. He was among those twelfth-century writers who aroused new interest in the Song of Songs. But his fresh interpretation of that biblical book was inspired by correlation of its text with personal experience.

> A book that I most recommend
> is the book of experience, my friend.
> Get the latest edition,
> for living tradition
> is worth it, whatever you spend.

"The book of experience" is Bernard's phrase, and by it he urges upon his monks the realization that Christ, prefigured by the Bridegroom in the Song of Songs, and memorialized in the Gospels, is discovered ever anew in the life of the spirit.

It did not escape Lethaby's attention that many fascinating new developments arose in the twelfth century, some of them orthodox, some heretical, some on the border. Lethaby was no friend of heresy, but he held that there was something inevitable about it in times of ferment and innovation. Somewhat like John Milton, he saw it as a kind of necessary byproduct to the reinvigoration of orthodox theology. Indeed, he even referred to a kind of necessary "balance of truth and error": there could be no advance in the articulation of truth, he thought, without a climate of fervid reflection and exchange that would inevitably produce much that would not pass muster, and the greater the intellectual and spiritual energy found in an era, the more it would produce of both error and truth.

If twelfth-century religious writing is rich and often surprising, that is also in part because the boundaries between theology, philosophy, moral exhortation, lamentation, and poetry were fluid, and the century expressed itself in all these modes and moods. Alan of Lille, for example, zigged and zagged across all the boundaries, and even when he was moralizing he did so with a sense of theological purpose.

> The world is a book for our reading,
> a picture with lessons worth heeding,
> and even a mirror
> – but all this is clearer
> to those who see where it is leading.

The original is slightly ambiguous: *Omnis mundi creatura/ quasi liber et pictura/ nobis est, et speculum*. This can mean either that "all the world's creation" is for us a book, a picture, and a mirror or that "each of the world's creatures" plays that set of roles. The context points toward the latter meaning: the very next stanza takes a particular creature, the rose, as teaching us the brevity of life. In other words, creation's lessons are clearest to those who already know the message, or more specifically to those who know that life leads toward death.

These twelfth-century writers were capable of as much doom and gloom as any others. Particularly famous for his lachrymose view of history and of life was Bernard of Cluny, who wrote page after page after page of dense Leonine couplets lamenting the world's decay:

> Where now are the cities of fame,
> whence heroes of splendor once came?
> The bloom once so rosy
> has withered; that posy
> is nothing except for its name.

Five lines in limerick, but only one line of a couplet in the original: *Stat rosa pristina nomine, nomina nuda tenemus,* or "The rose from of old stands in name, all we hold are bare labels." When Umberto Eco took this over for the ending of his novel *The Name of the Rose,* he broke it into two lines, but the original lumbers on lugubriously with its litany of lamentation in Leonine lines laced with internal rhymes.

Returning to Alan of Lille, he did not invent but did help a great deal to popularize what became one of the great conventions of theology:

> Our God is a mystical sphere,
> whose center is always right here,
> wherever we go!
> His circumference, though,
> has nowhere been sighted, I fear.

The usual formulation is that "God is an intelligible sphere whose center is everywhere and whose circumference is nowhere." The idea appears first in the anonymous *Book of the Twenty-Four Masters,* a twelfth-century work in the tradition of the legendary Hermes Trismegistus. From there it passed to Alan of Lille, to Saint Bonaventure, to Blaise Pascal, and many others, and has even been ascribed, oddly, to Voltaire. At least on one level, it serves as a way of talking about the immanence and transcendence of God, long before those terms became popular: as immanent to creation, God is centered everywhere; as transcending creation, God extends beyond it all. Jorge Luis Borges knew the idea from Pascal and developed it in his own fashion, even applying it to his phantasmagoric Library of Babel, with its interchangeable centers and its inaccessible periphery, again a source for Umberto Eco and *The Name of the Rose*.

The century that gave us the intelligible sphere also gave us Christian goddesses such as Nature, through whom God fashioned the world. Some writers of the age referred to Nature, Charity, Wisdom, and even Mary explicitly and unabashedly as "goddesses", plural figures who mediate the creative and formative energies of the singular God, as the many refract the potentiality and potency of the One. These writers did not get into trouble, because medieval religion was in some ways more open to daring formulations than we tend to suppose. This strand in medieval theology has only recently come to the attention of serious scholarship, but Lethaby did note it in Alan of Lille and others. Not surprisingly, he found it not to his liking. The goddesses of twelfth-century imaginative theology struck him as having been "just made up," and for him this was not a good thing. But the writers who gave us our conception of Nature were not troubled by these scruples.

> Natura can only complain
> that Silva is really a pain.
> She's still so chaotic,
> and slightly neurotic –
> she needs a makeover, that's plain.

In his *Cosmographia*, Bernard Silvestris has the goddess Natura come before the goddess Noys, complaining that Silva, or primal matter, is just a mess and needs to be licked into shape. Noys gets a team of goddesses to work on the project, and before long Silva is made into a properly ordered world. There are echoes here of Plato, with his Demiurge bringing order out of chaotic matter. There are also at least passing hints of the Bible. Bernard Silvestris could get away with his goddesses because he posed as a poet, however much he infused his poetry with theological insight.

At one point it occurred to me that the term "makeover" had a modern colloquial ring and might help me in dating the cycle of limericks. But no, it turns out that *Vanity Fair* as early as 1860 was talking about "Miss Angelica Makeover," who had coarse hair, "but by miracles of art and patience she has trained it into waves of beauty." Just like Silva.

Not everything was allowed in the twelfth century, and ecclesiastical dignitaries who felt their own authority challenged could be quick to cry heresy. Whence the following:

> You hierarchs may not wish to hear it,
> but spiritual folks need not fear it:
> the Father and Son
> and their ages are done –
> so clear out, and make way for the Spirit!

Medieval Christians were well familiar with the notion of two eras, one before Christ and the other begun with Christ's birth. Dating by "the year of the Lord" presupposed this two-era scheme of history. But if you take the time before Christ as the era of the Father, and the time inaugurated with Christ's birth as the era of the Son, what's left for the Holy Spirit? The monk Joachim of Fiore, writing in the twelfth century, suggested that the a third age was quickly approaching, that of the Spirit. There were corollaries to this schema. The age of married people had been succeeded by the age of clerics, which would soon in turn be replaced by the age of monks. The age of law had been followed by the age of grace, and now by an age of freedom and spiritual understanding. New religious orders would rise to prominence. The corrupt old Church would be replaced by a new, spiritual dispensation, which would be cause for rejoicing everywhere except perhaps in the palaces of popes and bishops.

Joachim's schema held great appeal in the generations after his death. He told people that they were living at a pivotal time in which exciting changes were destined to occur. This is a safe prophecy; change of some kind is always occurring. What made Joachim's version especially appealing is that the correlation with the Trinity – and there were other correlations as well – gave his view of history a definitive character. It was bound to happen, and the only surprise is that people hadn't seen it coming until Joachim told them. And once the third age came, it would be the last one, because there were only three persons in the Trinity. There was something satisfying about being on the cusp of the last and greatest phase in all of history.

What did arrive, shortly before Joachim's death, was the thirteenth century. It brought change, but not exactly what Joachim had foreseen: the blossoming of a theology quite different from that of the monks, that of the Schoolmen in their universities. Building on the work done in the cathedral schools, the university theologians of the thirteenth century produced great scientific summas, or compendia of theology, such as Thomas Aquinas's *Summa theologiae*. If you are trying to build a grand theological edifice, you need to lay the foundations, and that means, among other things, giving rational proof that there is a God.

It's apparent, and not at all odd,
that each motion is caused by a prod
from some previous motion,
which clinches the notion
that there's a Prime Prodder, called God.

Thomas elaborated "five ways" (*quinque viae*) for proving God's existence, but he thought the most manifest and straightforward was the argument from motion. (The arguments from causality and contingency are similar to it in form.) Imagine you come upon a billiards game just as a ball is going into a hole. It's possible that that ball was hit by another ball, which was hit by yet another, which was hit by still another, but sooner or later there has to have been somebody with a cue that got the process started. On a far grander scale, every motion in the universe is caused by some preceding motion. Thomas inherited Aristotle's view of the cosmos, in which motions on earth generally are stirred by motions in the heavens. Tides are the most obvious example, but Aristotle thought that indirectly *all* motion and generation can be traced to the movement of the heavenly bodies. If you are tracing a chain of motions back through previous motions, Thomas argues, you cannot have an infinite regress; sooner or later you reach a "Prime Mover", whom Thomas identifies as God.

Thomas did not think *everything* in Christian teaching could be proven rationally. For some doctrines, such as the Trinity, you needed the Bible's revelation. The Bible teaches also, in the very first verses of Genesis, that the world had a beginning and is thus not eternal. Could unaided human reason have addressed that issue? Many writers had tried, but Thomas thought they had failed; reason alone could not prove either that the world was eternal or that it was created, so for this too "revealed theology" had to rush to the aid of "natural" or rational theology.

Still, natural theology could be helpful on some of the most basic points, such as sorting out how it is possible to speak about God at all. It was Dionysius the Areopagite who gave classic form to the conundrum by suggesting that our human concepts, images, and vocabulary ultimately fall short and cannot apply to God. For Thomas, the key is the notion of analogy, or analogical predication.

> Health is found in a horse, yet we say
> that it's also in urine and hay,
> in a neither univocal
> nor quite equivocal
> deep analogical way.

Our language is usually about things that exist on a creaturely level, things we have learned about through our senses. God would seem to be different not just in degree but in kind from all these creatures. We know about good food and beautiful sunsets, but what could their goodness and beauty possibly tell us about God's Goodness and God's Beauty? If when we say "good" and "beautiful" we mean what *we* see in them, what proportion can their goodness and beauty have to *God's*, that the same words can apply to creatures and to God? Thomas answers by making a threefold distinction. We sometimes speak univocally, applying words the same way in different cases, as when we say that the sky and the sea are both "blue". At other times we speak equivocally, using words in fundamentally different ways, as when we speak of not just the sky and the sea but also our moods as "blue". There are still other times when we speak analogically. For this, Thomas's example is the health that is ascribed first of all to an animal, but then also to the medicine that is a cause of the horse's health, the food that sustains that health (not always part of the schema), and to the urine that the veterinarian holds up to the light and takes as a sign of the beast's health. So too, we *can* speak about God meaningfully by applying to him terms that apply also to creatures, and when we do that we are speaking analogically. We say that God and creatures are both good, meaning that the goodness in God, supreme and necessary, is the exemplar and cause of whatever goodness we find in creatures.

All the great schoolmen are known to history by titles befitting their character and interests: the Subtle Doctor, the Seraphic Doctor, and so forth. Thomas is known as the Angelic Doctor. This is a reference to his angelic sanctity, but it is further appropriate because the next great theme of the *Summa theologiae* after God is the angels.

> Seraphs, cherubs, bright thrones and dominions,
> Virtues, powers with shimmering pinions,
> Princedoms – archangels too! –
> and the angels' glad crew
> make up God's hierarchical minions.

Like others, Thomas saw the angels as hierarchical, and in this as in much else he was heir to the tradition of Christian Neoplatonism. For this tradition all creation was hierarchical, but most obviously the orders of angels. It had to be so, because the divine light is too bright for lesser creatures, and it must be received first by the seraphs, transmitted by them to the cherubs, and so forth on down to the lowest order of angels, who are called simply angels. As early as the second century, and on through the Middle Ages, Christians speculated about the "orders" or "choirs" of angels. Everyone agreed that the seraphim and cherubim came first, but after that it was up for grabs. The earliest list, in the *Apostolic Constitutions*, puts the "Aeons" in third place. Modern Christians may know the orders of angels from the opening stanza of John Athelstan Laurie Riley's hymn "Ye watchers and ye holy ones", which calls upon these orders – the bright seraphs, cherubim, thrones, dominions, princedoms, powers, virtues, archangels, and angels' choirs—to

44

join in praising God, as if they needed urging. While the limerick in our sequence follows Thomas Aquinas's hierarchy, with the positions of the virtues and princedoms switched, Riley goes instead with Gregory the Great.

The seraphim have special relevance to the work of Thomas's great contemporary Bonaventure. What Thomas was for the Dominicans, Bonaventure was for the Franciscans: their towering figure in thirteenth-century theology. But Bonaventure stood more clearly on the shoulders of his order's founder. While Saint Dominic, the founder of the Dominicans, enjoyed relatively modest veneration in the Middle Ages, Saint Francis quickly became a celebrity in medieval legend, art, and devotion. Shortly before his death, Francis had a vision of a crucified six-winged seraph from whom he received the wounds of Christ, or the stigmata, on his hands, feet, and side. This seraph called out for allegorical interpretation, and Bonaventure was happy to oblige.

> The wings of the seraph portray
> the stages that make up the way
> that leads up and above,
> where we know through our love
> the Creator we seek as we pray.

While Thomas Aquinas was in his own way a contemplative as well as a speculative theologian, the contemplative element is more fully manifest in the work of Bonaventure. The fusion of theology and prayer – the idea that the theologian speaks not only *about* God but also *to* God – had been commonplace in the early Christian centuries. It was less in the forefront in Scholastic theology, but it resurfaced in writers such as Bonaventure. Theology was not just an arid academic exercise, a way of making a career for yourself by marshaling clever arguments. It could be an exercise in contemplation, a questing for contact with God. But as the contemplative rises from one stage to another – symbolized by the six wings of the seraph in Francis's vision – rational and discursive exercise of the mind recedes, and loving contact with God moves to the fore. The relationship between knowledge and love cannot be reduced to stark contrasts, as though the Dominicans sought God simply through knowledge and the Franciscans through love. The best treatments of the matter make clear that mystical contact with God is always in a sense both knowing and loving, however much the emphasis and the precise relationship varied.

The conventional wisdom about Scholastic theology is that it developed through appropriation of the Aristotelian philosophy made newly available by a circuitous route, via translations from the Arabic. While rooted in biblical, early Christian, and Neoplatonic traditions, Scholastic theology made creative use of Aristotle as it evolved and matured in the hands of theologians such as Thomas Aquinas. It blended Aristotelian metaphysics and epistemology with earlier traditions. Different sources were useful on different issues, but they all proved helpful to the theologian. It was the Bible that proved the world was created and not eternal. It was the Neoplatonists who saw all creatures as reflecting eternal archetypes in the divine mind. But it was Aristotle who privileged sensory experience over ideas, and even the first three of Thomas's "five ways" prove God's existence from effects perceived by the senses—rather than from ideas, à la Anselm.

Bartholomew Lethaby had a rather different approach to this development. He too recognized that translations from the Arabic were important for Scholastic theology, but he saw the Schoolmen as quietly imbibing the mentality of the Arabic astrologers and alchemists. Like these practitioners of the occult sciences, the theologians were systematic in their speculation about matters that had little grounding in real experience. For Lethaby, the great Scholastic theologians were in essence theological alchemists. His reading was not entirely sympathetic.

Thomas Aquinas eventually came to be recognized as *the* authoritative theologian. As late as 1879, Pope Leo XIII declared that Thomas was mandatory reading in the seminaries. Because Thomas looms so large, it is easy to forget that there were numerous other Scholastic theologians who competed with him for attention, argued against some of his positions, and on some issues, such as the Immaculate Conception of Mary, came out in the end victorious.

> There once was a dunce called the Scot,
> who was no match for Thomas, with not
> even half his profundity,
> nor his rotundity.
> That's why he's nearly forgot.

But this is, of course, rather unfair. Duns Scotus has gone down as the original "dunce", but he actually made valuable contributions to metaphysics (with his emphasis on the "haecceity" or "thisness" – the irreducible particularity – of things), to Christology (he believed Christ would have become incarnate even without the Fall), and to Mariology (he was a major supporter of the doctrine of the Immaculate Conception, against doubters like Thomas Aquinas), and he made a deep impression on Gerard Manley Hopkins. And if Thomas was famously obese, Scotus's comparatively trim figure was surely not a vice.

Like Duns Scotus, William of Ockham was a Franciscan associated with Oxford. They were both willing to take risks, but Ockham was something more of a provocateur.

> The question may seem rather moot,
> but God *could* have been born as a brute,
> and if it were His will
> we'd be blessed when we kill,
> for his will still remains absolute.

This is Ockham in his most daring mood. Like other Scholastics, Ockham distinguished between God's absolute power and his ordained power. But he experimented with extreme formulations of that distinction. God created the world in a particular way, but he could have done it differently if he had willed. God chose to redeem humankind in a particular manner, but he could have done that differently, too, even becoming incarnate as a donkey. God chose to command that we should not murder or commit adultery, but if he had willed the opposite then *that* would have been good. Indeed, he could have commanded us to hate him. In short, everything hinges on God's will, which is subject to no restraints of reason. The way God has in fact arranged things is an expression of his ordained power. The way He *could* have arranged them lies within his absolute power.

Bartholomew Lethaby is not the only one to suggest a kind of affinity between Ockham's theology and the mysticism of his day. The mystics were far less technical, but they too challenged the power of reason and the authority of the Church. In extreme cases they were suspected of flaunting moral norms.

> "O virtues, I bid you adieu!
> What need could I have now for you?
> And however much it'll
> vex Holy Church Little,
> I say to my will, 'toodle-oo!'"

Marguerite Porete disseminated a dialogue called *The Mirror of Simple Souls*, which celebrated the annihilation of the soul. In an annihilated soul there is no more knowing or willing; God takes over and does all the knowing and willing on the soul's behalf. Still more astonishingly, perhaps, the annihilated soul has no more need of the virtues. And Porete exalted Holy Church the Great, whose members are the annihilated souls, over Holy Church the Little, populated by ordinary Christians. She was forbidden to spread this writing of hers, but she did so anyway, and thus she was burned at the stake in 1310, proudly disdaining to defend herself. For centuries, *The Mirror of Simple Souls* survived anonymously, and an English translation was even printed with an imprimatur in 1927. It was only in 1946 that the book was finally reunited with its author and scholars realized that this book with an imprimatur was the one whose circulation had brought Marguerite to the stake.

The better known mystic is Meister Eckhart, who was not burned at the stake but came close.

> Meister Eckhart was wont to remark
> that each soul is possessed of a spark,
> uncreated and godly.
> The pope, having oddly
> lost his, was just left in the dark.

Actually Pope John XXII condemned Eckhart's teachings as heretical, in 1328, just after Eckhart himself had died in prison. One of the most important of mystical theologians, Eckhart had preached and written about God, the soul, and the closeness of their affinity for each other. He never tired of finding new and striking ways to express the intimacy of God and the soul. To begin with, God's being is (for Eckhart) the only being there is, so any creature that has being has not its *own* but *God's* being. That is not to say that all things are God, because creatures have their particularities that make them porcupines and hedgehogs and hoopoes, but they are *existent* porcupines and hedgehogs and hoopoes by virtue of their share in the divine being. What distinguishes human beings from other embodied creatures is that they can be aware of this most intimate divine indwelling. Further, the human soul has within it a certain uncreated and thus divine something – a spark, a castle, a *je-ne-sais-quoi* – within which God lives and glows. To gaze within this uncreated chamber and see God glowing within it would be simply amazing and unforgettable and life-defining. It would be far greater than seeing, say, the Grand Canyon.

But if God is within each person, the reverse is also true: each person is within God. Following the Neoplatonists, Eckhart taught that there is an archetype of each person eternally present in God's mind, and that is the truest self of that person. You are most fully yourself not in time but in eternity, in God. Returning to the intense simplicity of your archetypal self – at death, but meanwhile through a kind of contemplative consciousness – is a breakthrough that lifts you out of your humdrum quotidian existence.

In all these ways, Eckhart spoke daringly, straining as best he could to impress upon people the intoxicating message of God and the soul dwelling within each other. Some people were deeply affected by Eckhart and his message and took him for something of a saint. Pope John XXII, a zealous administrator with few conspicuous marks of sanctity, was not among these admirers.

Not all mystics were suspect of heresy, and not all of them were marginalized. Nicholas of Cusa, the fifteenth-century mystical theologian, was one of the most abstract of them all, much given to mathematical analogies for his theology. It is tempting to speculate how he might have responded to non-Euclidean geometry and to relativity theory, given his interest in the *coincidentia oppositorum*, or the coincidence of opposites.

> When you've fought the good fight and then died,
> behind heaven's wall you'll reside,
> where black will be white
> and dark will be light,
> for opposites there coincide.

In his writing *On Learned Ignorance* he depicted God as dwelling behind the "wall of Paradise," where rational concepts cannot enter in, where impossibility coincides with necessity, and where contradictions generally coincide with each other.

Theologians in the universities could write condemnations and refutations of heresy, but they could also themselves be accused of heresy, sometimes for good reason. John Wyclif, a fourteenth-century theologian who studied and taught at Oxford, then went into service for the king of England. Like Geoffrey Chaucer, he functioned briefly as a diplomat. But his true calling turned out to be as a propagandist for royal causes, at a time when the king was eager to have theologians on hand to justify his intervention in ecclesiastical matters. That was enough to raise the eyebrows of other theologians, but Wyclif also challenged prevailing notions about the Eucharist and predestination. (He believed the substance of bread and wine remained, even when Christ became present within them.) Perhaps most important was his theme that "dominion" or authority, including that of bishops and other churchmen, presupposed grace. A sinful churchman was no real churchman. This teaching goes back to the Donatists of late antiquity, and Wyclif was not the only one to revive Donatist teachings. The practical consequence he drew was that the monarch would be justified in seizing Church property, which was not inconsiderable.

> Dominion is grounded in grace,
> so let's clean out our churches, and chase
> our bishops and monks
> – those spiritual skunks! –
> from the places their vices deface.

His teachings were condemned both at home in England and abroad, but he had powerful protectors, so it was only after his death that his bones were exhumed for burning.

The Schoolmen are often thought of as overly subtle and hair-splitting, a charge not totally without merit, although truer of some than of others. The cliché is that they occupied themselves with the question of how many angels can dance on the head of a pin.

> Just how many angels can spin
> in a dance on the head of a pin?
> When all's said and done,
> the answer is: none,
> because dancing is strictly a sin.

Did they in fact debate such matters? Perhaps not exactly, but a similar issue does arise ironically not in a Scholastic but in a mystical text, in a German work called *Schwester Katrei*. The holy woman Sister Catherine, like many saintly women of the later Middle Ages, is shown as having a devoted confessor who becomes her disciple. She has gone further than most of these holy women and is usually counted among the radical "free spirits" for which late medieval Germany was famous. Her confessor asks her to explain what "the masters," meaning the university theologians, have in mind when they say that a thousand souls in Heaven are able to sit on the point of a pin. She replies that souls do not occupy space or time, so of course you could get as many as you wanted into however small a space. As for the sinfulness of dancing, this was held by many early Christian writers, and it kept resurfacing. But it seems an unlikely concern for a free spirit.

Schwester Katrei is usually considered a heretical work, but not for its teaching on angels and pins. What did strike readers as heretical was her claim to have achieved such freedom of spirit and advanced so far in mystical union that she had become divine.

"My spirit is utterly free,
and I've soared to the highest degree.
I've been given the nod
and been turned into God.
Pretty good, for just little ol' me!"

Chapter 3

All Hell Breaks Loose: The Reformation and Counter-Reformation

The Reformation begins, at least for Bartholomew Lethaby and for the writer of our limericks, with Martin Luther's pamphlet of 1520 *On the Freedom of the Christian.*

> We're totally free, and in thrall
> to none, yet in slavery to all.
> We're not saved by our deeds,
> but by faith – yet that leads
> to a full and complete overhaul.

This pamphlet was a classic statement of Luther's views on grace, faith, justification, freedom, and bondage. The grace of Christ is offered to all, but only some have the capacity to respond in faith, to accept the fact that they are accepted, as Paul Tillich phrased it much later. Those who have this faith and can accept the grace offered are then sanctified, or transformed. They will perform good and holy works in the natural course of things. It is not the works that justify them, and yet works remain important for the disciplined life, lived according to God's will. Luther gives an analogy based on Matthew 12:33, that of the fruit tree: a good tree will spontaneously bear good fruit, and a bad tree will bear bad fruit, but you cannot make a bad tree good just by artificially attaching good fruit to it. Or taking freedom and bondage as the key terms, we are free from the law in the sense that it is not works of the law that justify and save us, yet still we have bonds of responsibility before God and toward our neighbors.

One might think this was not a radical message, and in some

respects it was not, but the implications of Luther's formulation were far-reaching. Among other things, the works that spontaneously follow from faith are mainly works of service and responsibility, not of asceticism or devotion. Faith may find expression in almsgiving and in preaching, but it does not lead a person to flog himself with a flagellum, to go on pilgrimage, or to endow works of ecclesiastical art and architecture. Because one either has faith or doesn't, and that simple distinction makes for salvation or damnation, without any middle path, there is no purgatory, thus no indulgences, no chantry priests to say masses for the souls of the deceased, no side chapels for these masses, no altarpieces piously commissioned for all these side chapels, and so forth. Luther's theology had sweeping implications for concrete religious practice. An entire edifice of pious and meritorious works came toppling down.

Luther won little favor with the traditionalist hierarchy or with the emperor, Charles V, but when he was condemned by the Diet of Worms in 1521, he was taken in by the Elector Frederick of Saxony in his castle at the Wartburg, where he kept busy translating the Bible into German and (as legend tells us) hurling inkwells at devils. Before leaving Worms, he famously declared that he stood where he stood and could do nothing else, "God help me. Amen."

> His fate here and after he ponders,
> while from Worms to the Wartburg he wanders.
> "They may get me tomorrow
> – but why should I sorrow?
> *Hier steh' ich - ich kann denn nicht anders!"*

It was only some years later, in 1533, that John Calvin felt himself called to reform the Church in France and published the first edition of his *Institutes*, a classic of Reformation theology that evolved through several editions.

> We're totally rotten, yet He
> unconditionally will decree
> case by limited case
> irresistible grace,
> as the saints persevering shall see.

The tenets of Calvinist theology, which began in France but took hold in parts of Switzerland and then in the Netherlands – are traditionally summed up in a formulation with the famous mnemonic device of TULIP, which stands for Total depravity, Unconditional election, Limited atonement, Irresistible grace, and Perseverance of the saints. We are all born in total depravity; as Augustine had taught with his version of the doctrine of original sin, and we all deserve the damnation to which we are fated. God decrees without setting conditions that certain people will be saved from that depravity and that fate, and these people are the elect, which is to say God's chosen ones. Christ's atonement is thus limited, not in the sense that it is imperfect, but in the sense that only some people and not all are able to benefit from its saving effect. Those chosen for salvation are given grace that they cannot resist. And being chosen to enter the ranks of the saints, they receive the power to persevere in grace until death.

Numerous further distinctions have been proposed within the Calvinist tradition: some have asserted that God's decrees of election and reprobation were "supralapsarian" (coming before the fall), while others have seen them as "sublapsarian" (coming after the fall). But the five basic doctrines have generally been taken since the Synod of Dort (1618-19) to define the essentials of Calvinist theology.

Calvin, like Luther, served not just as a theologian but as a reformer of the Church. Unlike Luther, who left secular juris-diction to the princes and magistrates, Calvin became involved in a project that blurred the lines of distinction between Church and state. The magistrates at Geneva called Calvin to implement his

Reformation in their city, and he worked closely with the civil authorities to ensure public morality.

No drinking, no dicing, no dancing,
no swearing, no cards, no romancing:
Geneva has banned
all vice from her land;
grim virtue goes gravely advancing.

The elect would take delight in serving God and in having every aspect of life kept under strict examination. That is not necessarily to say that they wanted the magistrates to come snooping in their own bedrooms, but if their neighbors were gambling or committing adultery it was always good to see them properly chastised.

The Anabaptists, meanwhile, moved off in a rather different direction.While the Calvinists sought to purge society of its vices, the Anabaptists withdrew into "gathered communities," separated from the mainstream, and refused to participate in its tainted institutions, such as its law courts and its armies. A fundamental problem with the Christian establishment, according to the Anabaptists, was the practice of infant baptism. If people are baptized before they can make a Christian commitment, the inevitable result is a church filled largely with uncommitted Christians. One Anabaptist pointed out that baptizing squirming infants before they can grow up and make a mature religious commitment is like washing vegetables before removing them from the soil.

Why baptize a newly-born squirt,
whose spirit and faith are inert?
That has no more merit
than washing a carrot
that's still planted deep in the dirt!

Actually the Anabaptist in question spoke not of carrots but cabbages, but the theological point is not vegetable-specific.

In England the challenge of the Reformers was to find a middle path between the extremes: the Roman Catholics wanted to preserve traditions passed down through the Middle Ages, while the Puritans, having absorbed Calvinist notions from the Continent, wanted to purge the English Church of all that was not clearly grounded in the Bible.

The "Elizabethan settlement", under Queen Elizabeth I, was a studied effort at compromise. Her majesty did not care a great deal how people interpreted their beliefs, so long as they were willing to live together in harmony, adhering to the famous "middle way" between the extremes. They could interpret the Eucharist in various ways, and when they prayed for their deceased loved ones they would not be asked whether such prayer implied a belief in purgatory. Her bishops and theologians were happy to comply with Elizabeth's desire.

> The queen would provide for her nation
> a stable dogmatic foundation.
> So let's give the lady a
> broad via media,
> paved with genteel moderation.

With the Roman Catholics, the Anglican Church preserved bishops and liturgical worship, with prescribed formulas and a liturgical year with its feasts and seasons. But with the Protestants they rejected papal authority and provided a simpler liturgy than that of the medieval Church.

Behind all the differences lay the question what sources Christians could draw upon in their quest for true doctrine. The classic Anglican answer to that question was formulated by Richard Hooker.

The bible, tradition, and reason:
that triad is always in season.
And if you should doubt it,
just don't go and shout it,
or soon you'll be suspect of treason.

Hooker's *Laws of Ecclesiastical Polity* first appeared in 1594, largely in response to the Puritan challenge to Anglican principles. Hooker has long been said to have based his theology on a "three-legged stool," the three legs being scripture, tradition and reason, or a "four-legged stool," the fourth being experience, unless experience is taken in conjunction with reason, in which case we are back to three legs, one of which is rational reflection on experience. In any event, the whole notion is an interpretive schema derived from Hooker, not without basis in his writings.

One of the most important issues for Hooker was the episcopacy. Like the Roman and the Orthodox Churches, the Anglican Church was governed by bishops, although without the tight centralized structure of the Roman episcopacy. The Puritans were in this as in other respects more radical than the Anglicans in their rejection of postbiblical tradition and in their repudiation of the Elizabethan Settlement, the established religious order worked out that had the queen's sanction and served the stability of her realm. They gave birth to two alternative polities: the congregational polity, in which each congregation is independent of external human authority, and the presbyterian polity, in which congregations cede authority to representative assemblies such as the presbytery.

Hooker found that the episcopal polity was grounded in Scripture, where there is explicit reference to bishops (or overseers), and the apostles themselves function in that role. Further, he appealed to the authority of tradition: the Church had always been governed by bishops. The notion that each bishop was consecrated by some previous bishop, on back to the apostles, is the doctrine of apostolic succession. Obviously there are more than twelve episcopal sees, or places governed by bishops, but that is because the apostles and their successors could consecrate increasing numbers of bishops as the Church expanded. Experience shows that having bishops is useful for maintaining due order within the Church. Hooker's reasoning is a particular application of his notion that the authority of Scripture must be taken along with the voice of the Church and with reason-honed-by-experience, all of which agreed on the key issue at hand, that the Church needed its bishops.

Many people have tried to explain why the Reformation took hold in certain lands and not in others. The most obvious factor is the political one: the principle established in Germany, *Cuius regio, eius religio*, meaning that the ruler gets to choose the religion for his territories, however large or small, was operative in other countries as well. But was it all politics and only politics? Bartholomew Lethaby thought it had to do mainly with wine. Places where wine was a mainstay of the economy, such as France and Italy and much of the Rhineland, remained Catholic. They needed all those masses for consumption of communion wine. Places furthest from the vineyards, like Scotland and Holland, went in for Calvinism. Places in between opted for more moderate forms of Protestantism, but still they went Protestant. Lethaby seems not to have considered in detail how countries like Ireland fitted into his picture. Perhaps he would have shrugged his shoulders and mused that to every rule there are exceptions.

The Roman Catholic response to the Protestant Reformers came in various forms, but the most definitive response of the hierarchy came at the Council of Trent, which met fitfully between 1545 and 1563. That council, like others, has come to stand for a great deal that was going on in the Church, whether it was directly connected with the council or not. Reference to the Council of Trent has become shorthand for the various Catholic reforms of the sixteenth century. So too in the twentieth century, people associate reforms of various sorts with the Second Vatican Council, even if they began well before that Council or took clear shape only in its wake. In the sixteenth century, the Council of Trent gave clear and public form to movements that had been simmering for years. It decreed a review of the liturgy, including the missal and the liturgical calendar, which remained basically in force for centuries. The adjective corresponding to "Trent" is "Tridentine", and people who grew up Roman Catholic before Vatican II might refer to the tradition of their youth as Tridentine Catholicism.

Fairly or unfairly, the Council of Trent has come to be seen as having a reactionary and rather strident character.

Faith is all that we need – and *that's it*?
Revelation comes only through Writ?
And the pope is a whore?
That's enough! Say no more!
Errant nonsense! *Anathema sit!*

The Council issued 33 canons on the doctrine of justification, and each canon takes the form, "If anyone should believe this or that error, let him be anathema." Likewise the canons on other subjects: they routinely end with *anathema sit*. Not content with blasting their Protestant adversaries, the Council fathers lit into each other as well, at one point there is said to have been a quarrel in which one participant tore the beard off the face of his adversary. The decrees, unlike the canons, had a more constructive flavor. Yes, they admitted, faith is the "foundation and root" of justification, the necessary beginning, the *sine qua non*, but a person who has been set on the right course by grace through faith can and should then experience an "increase of justification" by meritorious works. With similar subtlety, the Council reconciled the primacy of Scripture with the need for tradition as a supplement to Scripture. The Council did not actually take up the question whether the pope was the whore of Babylon, as Luther had charged, but it did seek to vindicate papal authority.

While the bishops and theologians were following the Council of Trent in all its many sessions, there were others in the Roman Catholic Church who had other matters on their mind, such as prayer.

> To water your garden, just go
> to a well – or if that seems too slow,
> use a wheel or a stream.
> But it works like a dream
> if it rains and the flowers just grow.

Teresa of Ávila was a nun, a reformer of monastic life, and a mystic. One of her mystical experiences has been immortalized in Bernini's statue of "Teresa in Ecstasy" in Rome. She is thus often thought of as the ultimate ecstatic, but the ideal she cultivated, the final stage in the mystical life, was a state of constant union or marriage with Christ in which ecstasies and raptures no longer play a major role. More than anything, she was a theologian of prayer, and one of her most famous analogies for prayer is watering a garden. You can water your garden laboriously by fetching water from a well. Less tiresome and more effective is using a water wheel. Yet easier and more efficient is having a stream running through your garden. But best of all is letting the rain fall directly onto your plants. So too, the earlier stages in the life of prayer call for much human effort, but prayer becomes easier and more effective as the individual who prays yields increasingly to Divine grace in action.

Teresa and her associate John of the Cross, another mystic and more of a poet than Teresa, exemplify the potential of the Catholic tradition for reform and spiritual vitality at precisely the time when many had given up on that tradition and turned toward one form of Protestantism or another. In later generations their influence was felt well beyond the Roman Catholic world. John Wesley, for example, was quite fond of Teresa.

At this point in the cycle of limericks there is one that appears at first to be out of place, and when I began working with the cycle I thought there was a problem with its transmission.

> There once was a serpent named Sam,
> who schemed the original scam,
> but, cursed then to slither,
> asked, "Who brought me hither?"
> And God thundered, "I did, Who Am."

This brings us back to the Book of Genesis, to the story of the Fall in chapter 3 of that book. Why does it come at this point in the cycle, just after the limericks on the Reformation and Counter-Reformation? Fortunately, Lethaby gives us the relevant clue. In his discussion of the Anglicans and the Puritans he mentions the huge impact their theology had on seventeenth-century poetry, and in that setting he mentions John Milton. Milton's *Paradise Lost* is famously a grand, panoramic effort to justify the ways of God to man by tracing the events of the Fall. The serpent tempter of Adam and Eve in Milton's version is Satan, otherwise sometimes known as Samael – whence "Sam". As the main rebel against God, Satan is a figure of heroic grandeur. Not coincidentally, Milton was a partisan of the revolutionary Parliament in the English Civil War, and he vigorously opposed restoration of the monarchy.

While *Paradise Lost* is a tremendously ambitious work of literature, Milton was not so ambitious for himself as its author; he accepted £5 payment for the first edition of 1667, with the provision that he would receive a bit more if further editions should prove necessary.

His main theological work, *De doctrina christiana* – if it was in fact his – was published only after his death, and it proved just as radically individualistic as anything else of his. He held that God is made of a kind of matter, that the three persons of the Trinity are not equal, and that God did not create the world *ex nihilo*. Bartholomew Lethaby, despite his disdain for anything that seemed to him made up, had grudging admiration for Milton because he took theology and its concerns very seriously indeed.

Chapter 4

Teetering on the Edge: The Modern Era

While the Reformers of the sixteenth century sought in certain ways to simplify Christianity by ridding it of complications they saw as untrue to Scripture, there were theologians of the seventeenth and eighteenth centuries who went much further in their simplifying, and they had much influence in the Enlightenment.

> The theists are in for a shock:
> the clockmaker just makes the clock,
> then leaves without tending,
> or mending, or sending
> some clue with each tick and each tock.

"Theists" were the traditional theologians. They believed in a God who, having created the world, lavished his providential care upon it. He performed mighty deeds, choosing his own people and smiting their enemies. He sent his Son to atone for sin, and he sent the revelation enshrined in the Bible. The "Deists" of the seventeenth and eighteenth centuries would have none of this. John Toland, who was among other things a biographer of John Milton, set forth these new theological principles in his book *Christianity Not Mysterious* in 1696. For Toland and the Deists generally, God was the great clockmaker who makes the clock and then leaves it to its own devices. They were persuaded that the order in the universe shows the ordering design of a wise creator. But they so no reason to believe in miracles, incarnation, redemption, or revelation. Their God was a purely transcendent one, off somewhere in the clouds, not an immanent one who cares about affairs on Earth.

The impact of Deism can be gauged from the shift it occasioned in theological language. Modern ways of talking about the transcendence and immanence of God came about largely in response to the Deist challenge. Augustine and Thomas Aquinas knew that God was present to creation, and of course they knew the creator infinitely exceeds the created order, but they did not use those as correlative terms. Insistence on the immanence of God responds to Deism, while emphasis on God's transcendence answers the pantheism which sees God as simply identical with the universe. Even in the early twentieth century speaking of God as "transcendent" in this sense could be referred to as a "modern phrase."

Bartholomew Lethaby saw the Deist movement as a paradoxical outgrowth of the Reformation. The Reformers of the sixteenth century sought to simplify Christianity, ridding it of those postbiblical excrescences of ritual, doctrine, and (to their mind) superstition that had cluttered true biblical religion, distracting and detracting from its purity. This emphasis was especially strong among the Calvinists and others who held that only what was in the Bible could be allowed in Christianity; Luther allowed for a generous category of *adiaphora*, matters of indifference, which included beliefs and practices that might not be found clearly in the Bible but still were not contrary to biblical teaching. In any event, the Reformers generally wished to rid medieval Christianity of purgatory and indulgences, all those devotional works that had been seen as garnering favor in God's eyes, needless ascetic rigors, and extravagantly spun-out legends of Christ and the saints. They were in all these ways the great simplifiers.

But now, says Lethaby, along came the Deists, who went even further and posed as even greater simplifiers. They got rid of miracles and revelations altogether, even those found in the Bible. Yet if in this way they might claim to go one better than the Reformers, in another way they reversed the direction the

Reformers had taken: dispensing with biblical revelation, they grounded religion solely on reason. Scholastics like Thomas Aquinas had sought a delicate balance between reason and revelation. Martin Luther, opting for a biblically grounded Christianity, had called reason the great whore. And now the Deists swung in the opposite direction, subordinating the Bible to rational religion. As Lethaby put it, the Deists were the children who turned on their parents. Before the Reformation their challenge to established authority would have met with little sympathy, but now they challenged the ground on which the Reformers had based their religion and gave preference to the ground that the Reformers had challenged.

A further unexpected twist came with the Jansenists, who remained Roman Catholic and retained a devotional and ascetic spirit that would have made Protestants nervous, but in their theology of sin and redemption they came close to Calvinism in a way that made most Roman Catholics uneasy. Their great opponents were the Jesuits, and one of the great scenes in Luis Buñuel's film *Milky Way* has a Jansenist and a Jesuit dueling with swords while carrying out a fierce theological debate. For our limerick writer, however, the Jansenist mainstream seems to have been less interesting than the thought of Blaise Pascal, the seventeenth-century Wunderkind mathematician and mystic.

> If God should exist, and you choose
> to believe it, you've paid him your dues.
> But if you're in doubt
> you might get left out.
> So try it – you've nothing to lose!

Pascal's famous wager is less an argument for God's existence than an argument for the reasonability of faith in God's existence. Pascal was not greatly impressed with metaphysical arguments generally: they are difficult to understand, and even when people have figured them out, their impact is fleeting. What did impress him profoundly was the human need for religion as a source of meaning in life. In his *Pensées*, or *Thoughts*, Pascal depicts the sorry state of a person without religion, who is likely to drift aimlessly and without any deeply felt sense of purpose. Others might have said that the Christian religion is true, and that recognition of its truth helps to make for a better life. Pascal said that in effect, Christianity helps make for a better life, and that its value for life is the main pointer to its validity. In this he is often seen as anticipating Christian Existentialists such as Søren Kierkegaard.

The Pascalian wager can be read in a narrow sense as referring to the requirements for salvation: if there is a God, and if there is salvation, then you cannot be saved unless you believe in God, so you stand to gain a great deal from believing, while if it turns out that there is no God and there is no salvation, you have still not lost anything by believing, so it's a safe bet. Within the context of the *Pensées*, however, Pascal is concerned not only with life after death: belief in God is what gives meaning and purpose to life itself.

If one wanted a general set of categories for understanding religious trends of the seventeenth and eighteenth centuries, one could do worse than to see a tug-of-war between claims of the mind and claims of the heart as the dominant theme. The Deists and their Enlightenment heirs, Voltaire and the rest, sought rational versions of religion, stripped of myth and superstition. The Pietists in Central Europe tended more to the requirements of the heart, and John Wesley made contact with the Pietist movement at a crucial point in his life.

> Wherever he preached, the crowds swarmed,
> and methodical classes were formed.
> They were so sanctified
> that their hearts nearly fried,
> though his was but curiously warmed.

In 1738 John Wesley attended a meeting in which a speaker read and commented on Luther's preface to Paul's epistle to the Romans. There can be very few biblical texts more often associated with religious conversion than the epistle to the Romans, so it is not surprising that Wesley's encounter with Romans brought about a kind of conversion experience. While the speaker was expounding the effects of faith upon a person's heart, Wesley felt his own heart "strangely warmed," and he gained assurance of his own forgiveness and salvation.

Central to Wesley's theology was the importance of gaining such assurance: "the plerophory or full assurance of hope," as he called it. One might perhaps be saved without this assurance, but typically and indeed as a norm it was expected for a Christian, and Wesley's preaching was calculated to produce it. Once equipped with this assurance, one might grow toward the perfection of "entire sanctification." Wesley rode about England preaching, often in the open air, to multitudes who, we are told, would groan and shout, swoon and fall to the ground, although Wesley himself remained "rocklike even when he seemed most on fire."

Wesley opposed the Calvinist doctrine of reprobation, the notion that some are predestined for damnation. His brother Charles Wesley, who knew well how to weave biblical and theological themes into densely eloquent and eminently singable hymns, shared John's aversion to Calvinist theology. Christ was for him the "general Saviour of mankind," whose "undistinguishing regard" was cast on all. The notion that the love of Christ is not freely available to all struck him as a "horrible decree," a "hellish blasphemy." Charles Wesley's hymns are full of emphasis that *all* may receive Christ's life, or that Christ may be expected to enter into the trembling hearts of all. In this he differed from Isaac Watts, the earlier eighteenth-century hymnodist who was faithful to Calvinist teaching, and believed that a volume "with all the fates of men" lies chained to the divine throne. The Wesleys stressed the importance of arousing religious emotion but then cultivating it systematically, methodically, hence the term "Methodist".

Their movement shared with the Puritans a form of preaching that began by inducing a sense of fear and sorrow for sin, then turning to the possibility of redemption, although Wesley and the Puritans differed in their sense of how far that possibility extended, and whether it is reserved for those specially chosen by God. In America, the Puritan preacher Jonathan Edwards was one of the best known practitioners of such preaching.

> Like a spider held over the fire,
> we'll perish through God's righteous ire,
> unless we repent
> ere this moment is spent,
> and the flames rise again all the higher.

Edwards delivered his most famous sermon, "Sinners in the Hands of an Angry God," in 1741. The biblical text for this sermon was Deuteronomy 32:35, "Their foot shall slide in due time." One would expect a Puritan, grounded in the broader Calvinist tradition, to emphasize the majestic sovereignty of God, and one is not disappointed on that score. But in two ways this sermon is particularly interesting. First, the key moment that Edwards chooses to linger on is not that in which the sinner goes to eternal damnation, but rather the moment *before* being damned.

Supreme in his power, God dallies with the sinner, dangling him over the fire like a spider. But second, there are exceptional times when the door is opened and it is possible for the sinner to embrace the Gospel, and Edwards claims his own day, and the revivalist "Great Awakening" that he did so much to inspire, as such an opportunity.

Preaching of this sort might have profound impact in the American colonies and on the frontier, but in places where people prided themselves on their high culture it might not ring so true. The educated high society of late eighteenth-century Germany clamored for a different style and a different message.

> Religion is based on a feeling
> of dependence that leads us to kneeling
> before the divine,
> infinite and benign.
> Now, isn't *that* gospel appealing?

For Friedrich Schleiermacher, the founder of Liberal Protestantism, the Christian religion is grounded not in rational propositions but in a *Gefühl*, or "feeling," or perhaps rather an intuitive consciousness, that we are all utterly dependent on "the Infinite," on God the benign creator and upholder of all things. That consciousness gives us a sense of connection not only with God but also with fellow mortals, who share our dependence. Christ came to humankind when its God-consciousness had waned, and he redeemed by teaching and showing what God-consciousness was meant to be. Schleiermacher first articulated this view of Christianity to its "cultured despisers" in 1799, addressing audiences who had turned away from religion either because it was too aridly rational or because it wasn't persuasive in its rational articulations. He was one of the first theologians who took it as his major challenge to win back those cultured individuals for whom the gospel no longer held any appeal, and who needed to be given a version of Christianity that did seem appealing and persuasive.

The notion was in the air that the rational foundations for religion were problematic and that some alternative was needed. For the Danish philosopher Søren Kierkegaard, religion is the third stage of existence to which one can rise. The aesthetic life is absorbed in a rather self-centered quest of pleasure. The ethical life submits to universally binding moral duties. But ultimately one must make a leap of faith and accept the religious life, in which ethical norms can be suspended or overruled by the demands that God makes not on everybody but on you in particular, just as he called on Abraham to be willing to sacrifice his son Isaac. Standing at the brink and preparing to make that leap of faith, the individual must confront the inevitable fear of the consequences, and indeed one of Kierkegaard's most important writings is entitled *Fear and Trembling*.

> From aesthetic delight and good cheer
> you can rise to the ethical sphere,
> and from there you can leap
> to religion so deep
> you'll be plunged into trembling and fear.

Ultimately Kierkegaard's message gained a real hearing in the twentieth century. In the nineteenth people were not quite ready yet for Existentialism, and the more influential voice was that of Schleiermacher.

Schleiermacher's exaltation of feeling made sense in the age of Romanticism, when poets, novelists, dramatists, painters, and composers were all paying tribute to the emotional life. But the Romantic movement fed a yearning for traditional forms of religion, for ritual and splendor, and this was rarely clearer than in the Anglo-Catholic movement of nineteenth-century England. Still, this Anglo-Catholic movement was not *only* concerned with ceremony and splendor.

> For an issue that's sure to be newsy,
> real presence is always a doozy.
> So is fasting... In fact,
> I could make that a Tract,
> or my name is not Edward B. Pusey.

Along with John Keble and John Henry Newman, E.B. Pusey was a founding leader of the Oxford Movement, which arose among clergy of nineteenth-century Oxford (its birth date is tradition-ally given as 1833). If there was any one core concern of the movement, it was the restoration of a sense of continuity with Apostolic tradition. Apostolic succession of the bishops was clearly important to that project, but so also were beliefs such as the real presence of Christ in the Eucharist, and practices such as fasting, which the adherents found in their reading of very early Christian literature. Such themes were promoted in the "Tracts for the Times," vigorously argued pamphlets that became widely read, influential, and controversial. The authors came to be known as Tractarians. Their contemporaries at Cambridge, founders of the Ecclesiological Society, were keen on the restoration of medieval liturgy, churches, furnishings, and vestments. The Tractarian movement at Oxford and the Ecclesi-ological movement at Cambridge served as foundations for the broader Anglo-Catholic movement in the Anglican Communion.

Bartholomew Lethaby's heirs have told me that he had some ties to the movement, although they could not be more specific.

> We're known for our smells and our bells,
> and our ritual sometimes repels,
> but our rites transcendental
> are more sacramental
> the deeper one enters and dwells.

Dominant among the Cambridge Ecclesiologists was John Mason Neale, the distinguished translator of early Christian hymns, who would probably not be pleased to know that he is remembered now mostly for his authorship of "Good King Wenceslas." For Neale and his associates, the principle of sacra-mentality was key to an understanding of church architecture and furnishings, as well as the rituals celebrated in churches. All true expression entails symbolic truthfulness, but sacramentality means investing that truth with "a greater force and holiness." It was not enough to build grand and intricately symbolic churches, and to hold aesthetically dramatic liturgies within them. Sacramentality meant entering more deeply into that symbolism and grasping the truth it contained. The point was perhaps lost on those who stormed out of churches where they found incense, candles, and Sanctus bells, or who initiated canonical proceedings against those who used the *Agnus Dei* or faced eastward during the consecration. The Anglo-Catholic movement evoked both keen devotion and vigorous resistance.

Anglo-Catholicism drew partly on medieval sources for ritual and its setting. Its adherents built Gothic Revival churches, they wore vestments in medieval design, they swung Gothic thuribles with various incense blends, and they were fascinated by the Sarum Missal that had been assembled in thirteenth-century Salisbury. An alternative source for their ritualism was the contemporary Roman Catholic Church, which exerted a magnetic influence on many members of the movement; some of its key leaders, notably John Henry Newman, went over to Rome. What distinguished Roman Catholicism most markedly from any branch of the Anglican tradition was its exaltation of the papacy as a force for cohesion within the Church. When you have a Church spread through the world, with members of all classes and temperaments, strong central authority can seem a useful hedge against factionalism, and the Roman tradition had a long commitment to central authority. Anglo-Catholics translated a great deal out of Latin sources, but the Romans continued to use Latin itself, for liturgy and for official business.

Formaliter dogmatizante,
de fide aut moribus fante
pontifice, ex
sese est lex,
nec populo tunc approbante.

In 1870, the First Vatican Council issued a dogmatic constitution on the Church, in which it formally defined the doctrine of papal infallibility. There were those who believed every time the pope opened his mouth he spoke infallibly, but that is not what the Council declared. Rather, it said that when the pope speaks *ex cathedra*, or "exercising the office of pastor and teacher for all Christians," and when he is addressing issues of faith or morals, his statements are infallible and irreformable in and of themselves, not from the consent of the Church (*ex sese, non autem ex consensu Ecclesiae*).

The last clause is directed against the Orthodox Christians who believed that official statements are not finally authoritative unless they have received general acceptance in the Church. The classic case is the union of the Eastern and Western Churches, accepted by the Council of Florence in 1439, but never accepted by the populace in Orthodox lands.

Our limerick writer makes of all this, "When the pope dogmatizes formally, speaking on faith or morals, he is a law in and of himself, even if the people do not then approve."

Why "the people" rather than the Church? John Henry Newman had published in 1859 an essay *On Consulting the Faithful in Matters of Doctrine,* in which he argued that the people of the Church generally are appropriately consulted prior to any dogmatic definition. There had been a survey of Catholic devotion before the official definition of the Immaculate Conception in 1856.

Newman pointed out that in the fourth century it was the people generally who adhered to the teaching of Nicaea, while

among bishops and councils "there was weakness, fear of consequences, misguidance, delusion, hallucination, endless, hopeless,
extending itself into nearly every corner of the Catholic Church."
The Holy Spirit may at times speak more through the faithful
than through their teachers. Newman saw consultation of the
faithful as appropriate *before* dogmatic definitions are issued,
which is not quite the same as the position that it is the people
who ratify a definition *after* it has been issued.

The pope who convened the First Vatican Council was Pius IX,
often referred to by the Italian as Pio Nono. At his election in
1848, he was thought of as having moderately liberal leanings,
but the revolutions of that year and the Italian Nationalists' threat
to the very existence of the Papal States soon left him and many
other Roman Catholics feeling embattled and disaffected. Pius's
Syllabus of Errors, issued in 1864, condemned pantheism, rationalism, indifferentism, socialism, communism, latitudinarianism,
naturalism, secret societies, liberalism, and much else, including
the notion that the pope and the Church should become reconciled with modern civilization.

> The whole modern world is our foe,
> and we really must shun the whole show.
> Can its liberal trends
> and tradition be friends?
> Pio Nono says no-no, you know.

Protestants could be just as keen on authority as Roman
Catholics, but for them the touchstone was a book, the Bible. Just
as Roman Catholics rallied around an infallible pope when they
saw their traditions under attack by the liberalism and other
movements of the nineteenth century, so too Protestants might
rally around an infallible Bible when they found Christianity
challenged by writers such as Charles Darwin.

Each word of the Bible is free
from error, and so too must be
each tittle and jot:
that's all that we've got
to keep apes off our family tree.

Belief in the inerrancy of Scripture could be found in Britain and in North America, but the movement known as Fundamentalism arose in America. It built on the teachings of conservative theologians such as Charles Hodge, who in the 1870s had written in defense of Calvinism and in opposition to Charles Darwin. The movement takes its name from a series of widely disseminated pamphlets called *The Fundamentals* (1910-15), and from a list of the "five fundamentals" first adopted by a Presbyterian assembly in 1910. The first of these fundamental doctrines was the inerrancy of the Bible in the original documents, and a corollary was a literal belief in the biblical story of creation, and thus a repudiation of Darwinist notions of evolution. But the rest of the fundamentals all had to do with Christ: his deity, his substitutionary atonement, his bodily resurrection, and his miracle-working power.

Belief in biblical inerrancy is not the same thing as biblical literalism. The Bible can be inerrant – absolutely correct, because after all it is directly revealed by God – even in places where it must be read nonliterally, as for example in the Song of Songs. What, then, about those biblical texts that refer not to the past but to the future: those that prophesy the end time, the second coming of Christ, the last judgment, and the great rapture? All these might be interpreted figuratively, or allegorically, but in conservative Protestant circles these texts tended to be read with meticulous literalism.

When signs of fulfillment imply
that the dread Armageddon is nigh,
with His great premillennial
coming – how many'll
find themselves rapt in the sky?

Christ lived, died, rose from the dead, and according to Luke's gospel and the Acts of the Apostles then ascended into heaven— but what then? Early Christians maintained a lively expectation that Christ would come again, perhaps in their lifetimes, this time in majesty, to judge all humankind. But the different texts predicting this second coming and last judgment – Matthew 24-25, I Thessalonians 4:15-17, Revelation 1:7 – seem to differ on points of detail. Some speak of a millennium of the saints, some refer to a great tribulation, and I Thessalonians in particular speaks of a rapture. How do these events fit together?

The simplest position, sometimes called amillenialism, holds that the millennium is not exactly a period of a thousand years but is simply a period of time corresponding to the history of the Church. At its end, all these events of Christ's second coming will occur more or less together. Next in order of complexity is postmillennialism, which holds that there will be a period of a thousand years when the saints will reign on earth, after which the events of the end time will occur. Distinct from this and more complicated is premillennialism, in which there is a great tribu-lation, followed by the second coming of Christ, followed by the millennium, all leading up to the last judgment. But those who read the Scriptures with a yet finer taste for fine points introduce a further stage in the process: first will come the rapture, or Christ's second coming *for* the Church, meaning those who will be lifted up into the sky to be with him; then the tribulation for those who are left behind; then Christ's second coming *with* the Church, which will inaugurate the millennium; and only then the last judgment. The second coming *for* the Church is not visible to all of humankind; it will involve a "secret rapture." But the second coming *with* the Church, and the last judgment, will be spectacular public events.

This last and most complex position is known as pretribulational (or dispensational) premillennialism. It is popular among certain American Evangelicals. It ascribes an especially prominent role to the rapture, which it sees as potentially imminent. But the position was articulated in the second quarter of the nineteenth century by the Anglo-Irish evangelist John Nelson Darby.

One of the keenest ironies in the history of Christianity is that the people who take an interest in you and make the keenest effort to understand you may in fact differ from you altogether in their own beliefs. William James, the Pragmatist philosopher, took a lively interest in Evangelical preachers and in the conversions they wrought with their preaching. If you claimed to have been born again as a true Christian, then James wanted to hear and retell your story. Yet his own philosophy was worlds away from that of the biblical literalists.

> Whether life is worth living depends
> on the liver – and therefore, my friends,
> you need not be naïve
> if your will to believe
> is a means to such practical ends

This reference to "the liver" is a famous pun from James's lecture "The Will to Believe," which he published in 1897. Is life worth living? That depends on the well-being of one's liver – or the attitude of the person faced with the question. How do we know that this is a moral universe, one in which it makes a real difference whether or not one lives morally? How do we know that we have free will, or that we are immortal, or that there is a God?

We have no empirical evidence of the ordinary sort to bear

out any of these hypotheses. But if we live our lives on the basis of these beliefs, we will find that we are living better lives. In his *Varieties of Religious Experience,* James had given numerous case histories of people whose lives had been powerfully improved by religious conversion. "The Will to Believe" went further, attempting to provide philosophical foundation for the reasonability of religious beliefs. Not their rationality, in the sense that they were subject to strict logical argument, but their reasonability. The test of belief was pragmatic, James was after all the great American Pragmatist. Truth in religious matters depends not on an abstract or fully objective standard. It hinges on subjective value to the liver, to the one whose life is lived and inspired.

By the late nineteenth century there was ample precedent for taking value-for-life as a criterion of truth, at least in certain areas. Immanuel Kant had concluded that God, freedom, and immortality could not be established by "theoretical" or "pure reason" but only by "practical reason": we know that we must live up to certain moral duties, whatever the consequences, and when we work through the implications of that conviction we find that it leads us to posit freedom, life after death, and God as the being who can and must bring goodness and happiness into their proper harmony.

One of Kant's followers simplified matters by articulating a philosophy of the "as if," meaning that God and freedom and immortality are not objectively real but we must live as if they were, and in Kant's posthumously published work there is already some warrant for this interpretation.

While religious beliefs for Kant were grounded in morality, Schleiermacher based religion on specifically religious intuitions, but for him too it was the need to make sense of human life that led to religious conviction. Søren Kierkegaard and the Christian Existentialists, again, found religion necessary as a basis for authentic life. Kierkegaard wanted not objective or absolute truth, but convictions that were true *for him*, truths he could live and die for. For the Scholastics, biblical revelation had stood alongside reason as an alternative *source* of truth; now religion became an alternative *kind* of truth, valid as a basis for morality or meaning in life.

Bartholomew Lethaby, of course, repudiated all these variations on the theme as so many ways of saying that the most fundamental tenets of the Christian faith are simply made up. He was particularly sensitive on this point. In any event, he did have interesting reflections on the course that many Christian theologians and philosophers followed in the century after Kant. He recognized this as a time when the natural sciences were coming into their own and beginning to show not only more solid theoretical grounding but also more pragmatic achievement. Chemists were able to serve the burgeoning industrial empires with improved and synthesized compounds from their test tubes, while biologists and physicians were on their way toward more accurate diagnoses, more effective preventions, and sometimes even cures. Theology had prided itself on being the queen of the sciences, but now it faced stiff competition.

Under these circumstances, Lethaby suggested, theologians tended toward a twofold strategy. First, they withdrew from competition altogether on theoretical grounds by renouncing all claim to the kind of merely objective knowledge that came out of the natural scientists' laboratories. Their truth claims were of a higher order. No one could expect them to rest upon the same foundations as the truths demonstrated in test tubes. At the same time, the theologians began to assert that their truths had practical effect far greater and broader than that of the natural sciences. The physicians might be able to innoculate against smallpox, but could they give meaning to life? The chemists might be able to produce synthetics of various kinds, but could they give proper grounding to moral values? The theologians thus opted out of one contest and declared themselves the winners of the other, on Lethaby's reading.

While German physicists and chemists pursued their experiments, the theology faculties of nineteenth-century Germany were famous for their development of biblical criticism. They applied to the Bible the tools of philological scholarship that had been used for classical texts. They asked how oral tradition came to be set down in written texts, how these texts came to be edited, and how historical and cultural circumstances found expression in the Gospels and other biblical texts.

This project gave rise to the original "quest of the historical Jesus" – as opposed to the second quest, located mainly in America, in the later twentieth century. Hermann Samuel Reimarus had suggested as early as the eighteenth century that Jesus was a failed revolutionary. Heinrich Paulus proposed in 1828 that the miracles of Jesus could be explained away in natural terms. David Friedrich Strauss in the 1830s published his monumental *Life of Jesus Critically Examined*, introducing a mythological interpretation of the gospels as a kind of Hegelian synthesis of orthodox supernaturalism and critical naturalism.

Albert Schweitzer inherited, analyzed, and extended this tradition of scholarship. For him, Jesus was not so much a failed revolutionary, but rather a failed apocalyptic preacher. He preached that the apocalyptic end of history was at hand, and after his death his followers expected that it would come at any moment. It didn't. They had to come to terms with this failure. For Schweitzer, the New Testament is the product of this apocalyptic fervor and its reinterpretation. One corollary to this emphasis on apocalyptic themes is that the rigorous morality preached by Jesus, especially in texts such as the Sermon on the Mount, must be understood as an "interim ethic," meant for that short and critical time left before the end of history.

> The ethical teachings of Jesus
> are far too demanding to please us.
> We'll give them a try
> if the end-time is nigh;
> if not, they do nothing but tease us.

If we have only a few weeks left, maybe we can turn the other cheek and give no thought to where our next paycheck will come from. The ethic applies less clearly to the long haul, Schweitzer suggests.

This world of German theological scholarship seems to be the world that Bartholomew Lethaby's publishers Hans Spassvogel and Johannes Griesgram came from, although their interest in Lethaby suggests that they had perhaps repudiated the rationalism of nineteenth-century German biblical scholarship when they established their firm in London.

One hears vague and undocumented reports that of the two partners in the publishing house one was more sympathetic toward Lethaby than the other. If this is true, it is tempting to speculate that some of the tensions found in the world of German scholarship are reflected in their publishing agenda, although documenting that hypothesis might well prove difficult.

In any event, German biblical scholarship retained its hegemony well into the twentieth century, and one of the most influential of all twentieth-century biblical scholars was Rudolf Bultmann.

> The Bible is marked with a stigma:
> its myths are a *frightful* enigma.
> But still, don't apologize,
> just demythologize –
> saving, of course, the kerygma.

Bultmann is unusual among major theologians in the degree to which he combined theology with textual biblical scholarship. His "form criticism" was influential in twentieth-century endeavors to see how the gospels were pieced together from originally distinct units. More radical was his insistence that the gospels are not historical documents but contain myths, stories meant to convey an underlying *kerygma*, or message. The theologian must learn to demythologize the gospels, stripping away the mythic narrative, to get at the heart of Jesus's teaching – which just happens to be a version of the Existentialist philosophy propounded by Martin Heidegger, a colleague of Bultmann's. This was the basis for Bultmann's effort to identify the theological and philosophical, if not historical, core of the gospels.

The Swiss theologian Karl Barth was brought up in the tradition of Liberal Protestantism, and in some ways remained indebted to it, but his Neo-Orthodoxy emerged out of a sense, during and after World War I, that Liberalism was insufficient. He now reread the Bible, he said, not from a human standpoint but from the standpoint of God. And his view of God was deeply informed by his Calvinist heritage: God is utterly sovereign, powerful over all creation, free above all human categories. This meant rejecting the Liberal attempt to find warrant for Christian doctrine in human experience, and it meant also rejecting any version of the Scholastic attempt at "natural" or rational theology. God does not submit to human logic.

Barth's fellow Swiss theologian Emil Brunner modestly proposed a limited recovery of natural theology, suggesting that the analogy of being, the *analogia entis*, could rehabilitated: it might be possible to discern some analogy or proportion between God's being and creatures' being, which then could become the basis for further connection between God and creatures. Barth's response was a thundering refutation, in the form of a pamphlet entitled, simply, *Nein! (No!)*

"*Analogia entis*," said Barth,
"Is a notion more daring than smart.
When it comes to religion,
we know not a smidgen
beyond what God wills to impart."

Years later, Brunner was said to quiver whenever reminded of this exchange.

Of course he is free to opine
what he will on these matters divine.
But can't he forego
these anathemas? No,
I fear that the answer is *Nein!*

While Barth insisted on beginning with God's point of view rather than the human vantage point, the privilege of a human starting-point for theology gained new life in the Christian Existentialism of Paul Tillich.

Just think of your highest concern,
and from it you'll quickly discern
that the Ground of all being
is God, guaranteeing
the meaning for which we all yearn.

Tillich was born in the same year as Barth, 1886, but there the similarities more or less end. Tillich began with a keen sense of the human situation with all its misery, its precariousness, its sense of finitude and potential futility. If life is so fragile that it could be snuffed out at any moment, then what reason do we have to celebrate it as something genuinely valuable? We may cast our lot with the atheist Existentialists and say that the meaning and value of life is ours to determine, and that we must do so freely, unconstrained by anyone's notions of who we are or what we are obliged to do. For Tillich, this is making oneself into God, and it becomes a source of frustrated alienation. Instead, we must gain contact with the depth dimension of our life, the Ground of our being. We may or may not profess to believe in God, but if we acknowledge that life has depth, then we are not genuinely atheists. We find that we have an "ultimate concern," which gives meaning to our lives. That ultimate concern, that Ground of being, can be called God, but it need not go by that name. While Barth takes the Bible in principle as his starting point and works out the implications of biblical revelation, Tillich begins with cultural expressions of human experience, with the arts and the sciences and current affairs, and he then "correlates" the Gospel with these, making it an answer to the human situation.

Tillich's interest in contemporary culture as a starting point for theology led him to an interest in different kinds of culture, and different ways culture related to religion.

> The culture of Christian theonomy
> yields to a grim heteronomy,
> then, by a sceptic-
> al new dialectic,
> it founders on human autonomy.

Perhaps more than any other notion in the history of theology, Paul Tillich's theory of religion and culture was made to be turned into a limerick. Fundamentally, this notion of history is cyclical. In a culture of theonomy, spiritual values lie at the very heart of cultural expression, and people spontaneously express themselves in spiritual terms. In a culture of heteronomy, spiritual values are imposed from outside. And in a culture of autonomy, people claim that they themselves create values, until eventually they come around, as in the shift from the Renaissance to the Reformation, and theonomy is revived.

While Tillich was attempting to reinterpret and give new meaning to Christian beliefs, he was willing to dispense with the very term "God", to see God as more absent than present from his age, and to recognize that many Christian notions are now "broken myths" and can no longer be accepted as they once were. In these ways he prepared the ground for the proclamation in the 1960s that God is dead, a movement that harked back to Friedrich Nietzsche's book *The Gay Science*, in which a madman rushes into the marketplace and alarms everyone with the panicked declaration that God is dead, and indeed humankind itself has killed him with its knives.

> Some people think God is now dead.
> "We killed him!" the madman has said.
> But the madman is crazed:
> He's not dead, He's just dazed,
> and soon He'll spring up from his bed.

Once again, as in the writings of Anselm of Canterbury, the atheist is depicted as mentally deranged. But Anselm's fool, borrowed from the Psalms, is merely wrong on a point where being right is all-important. Nietzsche's madman is deranged because he realizes the magnitude of what Western culture has done in killing off the concept of God and thus decentering civilization and its values. The deed may from one perspective seem heroic, but still Nietzsche and his madman recognize that the consequences will not be easily borne.

This seems to be the last word for the writer of our limericks, who obviously drew on sources later than Lethaby's book but none later than the 1960s. Like so many, the limerick writer seems thus to be a product of the sixties, which no doubt accounts for a great deal, for better or for worse. Rarely has there been a decade that has cast so long a shadow over the culture of succeeding decades, challenging previous culture but serving as a wellspring for later generations to draw upon, stimulating the imagination in ways that do not quickly grow irrelevant. Whatever we make of that decade and its theology, we can be reasonably certain that Bartholomew Lethaby would not have found it to his liking.

It was during the sixties that I like many of my contemporaries first began reading theology – Rudolf Bultmann and Paul Tillich, Romano Guardini and Karl Rahner – and when Rahner came to town I got to hear his opinion of the latest decree from the Vatican.

One of my teachers urged me to open an account with Blackwell's bookstore, suggesting that was the best way to get books in German, and so I did. Which is how, in late adolescence, I found myself working through Joachim Jeremias's *Die Gleichnisse Jesu*. Years later, when I first went to Oxford, a visit to Blackwell's on Broad Street had something of the feel of a pilgrimage.

In Blackwell's, I found an extensive section of Secondhand Theology, and for a moment I wondered what sort that might be. That was the day when looking for used book was an adventure; finding any particular book in the shops and the catalogues might be a hopeless quest, but one never knew what might turn up along the way. Entire bookshelves in one's library could be filled with books that looked as if they might some day be useful and might never again be available if one didn't snap them up now. With the Internet, all that has changed. It takes just seconds to find multiple copies of the same book, ranging wildly in price. Still, when the book arrives it can still be an adventure, because every book contains much that the reader never expected. Indeed, sometimes even the author, because one never knows what will show up tucked into the pages of one's own book.

Notes

Chapter 1

page 5-6: The passage quoted from Irenaeus is in *St. Irenaeus of Lyons Against the Heresies*, Book 1, Chapter 11, trans. Dominic J. Unger, rev. John J. Dillon, vol. 1 (New York and Mahwah, N.J.: Paulist Press,), pp. 52-53.

page 6-7: The analogy of the prism and the magnifying glass is suggested in Richard Kieckhefer, *Theology in Stone: Church Architecture from Byzantium to Berkeley* (New York: Oxford University Press, 2004), 84. Crucial to this imagery is that it is the same light-source, the sun, which is in the one case refracted and in the other focused.

pages 10-15: For the documenst of all these early councils, see *Decrees of the Ecumenical Councils*, ed. Norman P. Tanner, with original texts established by G. Alberigo, et al. (London: Sheed & Ward; Washington, DC: Georgetown University Press, 1990), vol. 1: the creed of Nicaea, 5; its revised version from the First Council of Constantinople, 24; the formula of union at Ephesus, 69-70 (cf. 71); the definition of the faith at Chalcedon, 82-87.

page 14: C.S. Lewis discusses the relationship between pagan myth and Christian doctrine in *Surprised by Joy: The Shape of My Earthly Life* (London: Bles, 1955; repr. New York: Harcourt, 1995), 62-63, 78, 166-67, 223-24, and especially 235-36. For mythology in Lewis, see his oeuvre, *passim*.

page 15: The limerick on Augustine's *Confessions* actually combines three key passages: the theft of the pears, motivated by peer pressure, in book 2, chap. 4; the plea for postponed chastity in book 8, chap. 7; and the more general petition for grace in book 10, chaps. 29 (twice), 31, 37. See Saint Augustine, *Confessions*, trans. R.S. Pine-Coffin

(Harmondsworth: Penguin, 1961), 47-78, 169, 233, 236, and 245.

page 18: There is also a letter of Pseudo-Augustine in which a voice speaks to the saint from a burst of light, asking if he thinks he can empty the sea into a small bottle. Sources are discussed in Henri-Irénée Marrou, "Saint Augustin et l'ange: Une légende médiévale," in *L'Homme devant Dieu, Mélanges offerts au P. de Lubac*, vol. 2 (Paris: Aubier, 1964), 137-49, and in Jeanne Courcelle and Pierre Courcelle, *Iconographie de Saint Augustin: Les cycles du XVe siècle* (Paris: Études Augustiniennes, 1969), 100-01 and 104.

pages 19-20: B.A.G. Fuller, *The Problem of Evil in Plotinus* (Cambridge: Cambridge University Press, 1912); Christian Mofor, *Plotinus and African Concepts of Evil : Perspectives in Multi-Cultural Philosophy* (Bern and New York : P. Lang, 2008).

pages 20-21: Arthur Schopenhauer, *The World as Will and Representation*, trans. E. F. J. Payne (New York: Dover, 1966).

pages 21-22: Pseudo-Dionysius, *The Complete Works*, trans. Colm Luibheid (New York: Paulist, 1987), includes editions of *The Divine Names*, with the three ways of conceiving the motion of "divine intelligences" or angels (chap. 4, sect. 8, p. 78), with parallel description of the motions of the soul (chap. 4, sect. 9, p. 78) and of God (chap. 9, sect. 9, p. 119). The volume also contains *The Mystical Theology* (pp. 135-41).

pages 22-23: The material from Boethius is in *The Consolation of Philosophy*, Book 2, Poem 8, trans. Richard Green (New York: Macmillan, 1962), 41.

page 23: San Pietro in Ciel d'Oro, in Pavia, claims the relics of Augustine in its choir and (with perhaps greater plausibility) Boethius in its crypt. Relics or no relics, the church repays a visit. See Benedict Hackett, "San Pietro in Ciel d'oro, Pavia," in Joseph C. Schnaubelt and Frederick Van Fleteren, eds., *Augustine in Iconography: History and Legend* (New York: Peter Lang, 1999), 199-222, and Harold Samuel Stone, *St. Augustine's*

Bones: A Microhistory (Amherst: University of Massachusetts Press, 2002).

page 24: The literature on the Seven Deadly Sins is almost as abundant as the sins themselves. See, for example, Solomon Schimmel, *The Seven Deadly Sins: Jewish, Christian, and Classical Reflections on Human Psychology* (New York: Oxford University Press, 1997).

pages 24-25: Jerome's apology for marriage is in his Letter 22, to his disciple Eustochium, sect. 20. See *Select Letters of St. Jerome*, trans. F. A. Wright (Cambridge, Mass.: Harvard University Press ; London: Heinemann, 1980), 94-95: *Laudo nuptias, laudo coniugium, sed quia mihi virgines generant.* One might be pardoned for seeing an element of self-centeredness in Jerome's suggestion that marriage was breeding more virgins specifically for him. The notion that God brings good out of evil is found in Augustine, e.g., *Sermones de Scripturis*, 61, c. 2, *Patrologia Latina*, 38 (Paris: Migne, 1841), 409: *Sed qui semper est bonus, ipse facit ex malo bonum.* Thomas Aquinas in his *Quaestiones disputatae de potentia* (for which there is an on-line translation), qu. 3, art. 6, ad 4, represents God as so powerful that he can draw good from any evil (*de quolibet malo posset elicere bonum*).

page 25: Tertullian, "On the spectacles," chap. 30, in Tertullian's *Disciplinary, Moral, and Ascetical Works*, trans. Rudolph Arbesmann, Sister Emily Joseph Daly, and Edwin A. Quain (New York: Fathers of the Church, 1959), 104-07. Tertullian's prose itself had something of a spectacular quality to it.

Chapter 2

page 28: For a discussion of how allegory functioned, see Jon Whitman, *Allegory: The Dynamics of an Ancient and Medieval Technique* (Cambridge, Mass.: Harvard University Press, 1987).

pages 29-32: Anselm of Canterbury, *The Major Works*, ed. Brian Davies and Gill Evans (New York: Oxford University Press, 1998), gives the *Proslogion* (the source for the ontological argument, chap. 2, pp. 87-88) and *Why God Became Man* (where Anselm articulates his theory of atonement, pp. 260-356).

page 33: On the four daughters of God and especially the formulation by Robert Grosseteste, see Barbara Newman, *God and the Goddesses: Vision, Poetry, and Belief in the Middle Ages* (Philadelphia: University of Pennsylvania Press, 2002), 44-47

pages 33-34: Cuthbert Butler discusses the classic tension between the ideals of action and contemplation, as articulated by Augustine, Gregory the Great, and Bernard of Clairvaux, in *Western Mysticism: The Teaching of Augustine, Gregory and Bernard on Contemplation and the Contemplative Life*, Part II, 3rd ed. (London: Constable, 1967), 157-223.

pages 34-35: When I inquired whether *Sic et non* has ever been translated into English, the answer was "No...yes!" One might begin with Jeffrey E. Brower and Kevin Guilfoy, eds., *The Cambridge Companion to Abelard* (Cambridge: Cambridge University Press, 2004).

page 36: On the importance of experience (especially for Bernard) see Jean Leclercq, *The Love of Learning and the Desire for God: A Study of Monastic Culture*, trans. Catharine Misrahi (New York: Fordham, 1961), 5 and 211-17.

pages 37-38: For the lines from Alan of Lille, see G.R. Evans, *Alan of Lille: The Frontiers of Theology in the Later Twelfth Century* (Cambridge: Cambridge University Press, 1983), 151.

page 38: The famous line about the withering rose is in *Scorn for the world: Bernard of Cluny's* De contemptu mundi, book 1, line 952, ed. and trans. Ronald E. Pepin (East Lansing, Mich.: Colleagues Press, 1991), 68-69. It comes at the very end of Umberto Eco, *The Name of the Rose*, trans. William Weaver (San Diego: Harcourt Brace Jovanovich, 1983); the film version throws in the towel on this reference, turning "Rose" into the implied name of the strumpet. The capacity of twelfth-century writers for doom and gloom is explored in C. Stephen Jaeger, "Pessimism in the Twelfth-Century 'Renaissance'," *Speculum*, 78 (2003), 1151-83. Pepin's edition substitutes *Roma* for *rosa* on the strength of a single early manuscript reading. But all the other manuscripts give *rosa*, and in context *rosa* is the *lectio difficulior* (i.e., it is easy to see how a scribe could mistake *rosa* for *Roma*, but the reverse is harder to envision). Besides which, elsewhere in the poem, even shortly before the passage in question, Bernard uses rose imagery (bk. 1 lines 883 and 896, bk. 2 line 915, bk. 3 line 106; cf. bk. 1 line 810, bk. 2 line 374).

pages 38-39: The theme of the intelligible sphere is mentioned in Andrew Weeks, *German Mysticism from Hildegard of Bingen to Ludwig Wittgenstein: A Literary and Intellectual History* (Albany: State University of New York Press, 1993), 106.

pages 39-40: Bernardus Silvestris, *The Cosmographia*, trans. Winthrop Wetherbee (New York: Columbia University Press, 1973); see also Newman's *God and the Goddesses*, 55-65. Newman's book deals generally with medieval notions about God and the mediating role of goddesses. One might say the goddesses are mere allegories, but the point is, largely, that there is no such thing as "mere" allegory.

pages 40-41: Bernard McGinn, *The Calabrian Abbot: Joachim of Fiore in the History of Western Thought* (New York: Macmillan, 1985), 161-203.

pages 41-43: For Thomas Aquinas's five proofs for the existence of God, see his *Summa theologiae*, pt. 1, qu. 2, art. 3, translated in *Introduction to St. Thomas Aquinas*, ed. Anton C. Pegis (New York: Modern Library, 1945), 24-27; the argument from motion (the "first and most manifest way") is on p. 25. For the doctrine of analogy, the classic source is the *Summa theologiae*, pt. 1, qu. 13, especially art. 5, given in Pegis's translation on pp. 106-09

page 44: Bonaventure, *The Journey of the Mind to God*, trans. Philotheus Boehner, ed. Stephen F. Brown (Indianopolis: Hackett, 1993). For the role of love in the mysticism of Bonaventure and other writers, see Bernard McGinn, "Love, knowledge, and mystical union in Western Christianity: twelfth to sixteenth centuries," *Church History*, 56 (1987), 7-24.

page 47: Arthur Cushman McGiffert, *A History of Christian Thought*, vol. 2 (New York: Scribner, 1933), 297, comments wryly, "To read Thomas is a delight; to read Duns is a weariness to the flesh." The poetry of Hopkins is actually not a bad starting point for exploring Duns Scotus. See Bernadette Waterman Ward, *World as Word: Philosophical Theology in Gerard Manley Hopkins* (Washington, D.C.: Catholic University of America Press, 2002), Chap. 7, "Duns Scotus: *formalitas* and inscape," 158-97.

pages 47-48: Ockham's daring formulations are in his *Centilogium* (eg.conclusion 7) and his *Quaestiones in quattuor libros sententiarum* (eg., ii, qu.19). But see the cautionary remarks by Marilyn McCord Adams, "Ockham on will, nature, and Morality," in Paul Vincent Spade, ed., *The Cambridge Companion to Ockham* (Cambridge: Cambridge University Press, 1999), 245-272.

pages 48-49: Marguerite Porete, *The Mirror of Simple Souls*, trans. Ellen L. Babinsky (New York: Paulist, 1993). The soul takes leave of the virtues in chapter 6. The wording "toodle-oo!" is probably the greatest poetic license in this cycle, capturing nothing of Porete's diction.

pages 49-50: Bernard McGinn, *The Mystical Thought of Meister Eckhart: The Man from Whom God Hid Nothing* (New York: Crossroad, 2001).

pages 50-51: Jasper Hopkins, *Nicholas of Cusa's Dialectical Mysticism: Text, Translation, and Interpretive Study of De visione Dei* (Minneapolis: Arthur J. Banning Press, 1985). The theme of the wall of Paradise (*murus paradisi*) is introduced in chap. 9, pp. 160-61.

page 51: Matthew Spinka, ed., *Advocates of Reform, from Wyclif to Erasmus* (Philadelphia: Westminster, 1953), 21-60.

pages 52-53: "The 'Sister Catherine' Treatise," trans. Elvira Borgstädt, is in Bernard McGinn, ed., *Meister Eckhart: Teacher and Preacher* (New York: Paulist, 1986), 347-87.

Chapter 3

page 54: Martin Luther's fundamental work "The Freedom of a Christian" is in *Three Treatises*, rev. ed. (Philadelphia: Fortress, 1970), 277-316.

pages 55-56: David N. Steele, Curtis C. Thomas, and S. Lance Quinn, *The Five Points of Calvinism Defined, Defended, Documented*, 2nd ed. (Phillipsburg, N.J.: P & R Publications, 2004).

pages 57-58: For the reference to washing unharvested cabbages, see Roland H. Bainton, *The Penguin History of Christianity*, vol. 2 (Harmondsworth: Penguin, 19964), 134. One might argue that carrots work better than cabbages, because carrots actually do grow in the ground, while cabbages do not.

pages 58-59: Hooker discusses the episcopacy in his *Laws of Ecclesiastical Polity*, book 7, given in *The Works of that Learned and Judicious Divine Mr. Richard Hooker, with an Account of His Life and Death by isaac Walton*, ed. John Keble, 4th ed., vol. 3 (Oxford: 1863), 140-325.

pages 60-62: For the documents of Trent, see *Decrees of the Ecumenical Councils*, ed. Tanner, vol. 2, 660-799 (the decree on justification, 671-78; the canons, 679-81).

page 62: Teresa of Ávila's garden imagery is in her autobiography, Chap. 11, given in *The Complete Works of Saint Teresa of Jesus*, trans. and ed. E. Allison Peers, vol. 1 (London and New York: Sheed & Ward, 1957), 65-70.

page 63: On the identity of Samael and Satan see, e.g., Robert H.

West, *Milton and the Angels* (Athens: University of Georgia Press, 1955), 156. The extensive article in Gustav Davidson, *A Dictionary of Angels, Including the Fallen Angels* (New York: Free Press, 1967), 255, explains that the name Samael means "poison-angel".

Chapter 4

page 65: John Toland, *Christianity Not Mysterious* (London, 1696; repr. New York: Garland, 1978).

page 66: For the point about immanence and transcendence, see Richard Kieckhefer, "Immanence and transcendence in church architecture," *Koinonia: The Journal of the Anglican & Eastern Churches Association*, New Series No. 54 (All Saintstide 2008), 29-40. The key argument here is against the widespread but perverse notion that an architecture of splendor is somehow naturally associated with divine transcendence, while a more modest architecture is a sign of divine immanence.

pages 67-68: For Pascal's wager see the *Pensées*, XLV ("Discourse concerning the machine"), sect. 680, in Blaise Pascal, *Pensées and Other Writings*, trans. Honor Levi (Oxford: Oxford University Press, 1995), 154-55.

pages 68-69: The account of Wesley's heart being "strangely warmed" is in Wesley's journal for May 24th, 1738, given in *The Works of the Rev. John Wesley*, 3rd American ed., vol. 3 (New York: Carlton & Phillips, 1853), 74. A.H.M. Lunn contrasts Wesley's preaching with that of George Whitefield: Whitefield "was the captive of the forces which he set in motion. Wesley, on the other hand, remained calm and even critical, when the thousands around him were in the throes of revival fever." See Arnold Henry Moore Lunn, *John Wesley* (London: Cassell, 1929), 114, quoted in R.A. Knox, *Enthusiasm: A Chapter in the History of Religion, with Special Reference to the XVII and SVIII Centuries* (Oxford: Clarendon, 1950), 515.

pages 69-70: For the contrast between Watts and Wesley, see Albert Edward Bailey, *The Gospel in Hymns: Backgrounds and Interpretation* (New York: Scribner, 1950), Chaps. 4 and 5.

page 71: Friedrich Schleiermacher, On Religion: Speeches to Its Cultured Despisers, trans. Richard Crouter (Cambridge: Cambridge University Press, 1988).

page 72: Søren Kierkegaard, *Fear and Trembling: Dialectical Lyric by Johannes de Silentio*, trans. Alastair Hannay (Harmondsworth, Middlesex: Penguin; New York: Viking Penguin, 1985); and *Either/Or*, ed. and trans. Howard V. Hong and Edna H. Hong (Princeton, N.J.: Princeton University Press, 1987).

pages 72-73: William G. Hutchison, ed., *The Oxford Movement: Being a Selection of Tracts for the Times* (London: Scott, 1906).

pages 73-74: Michael Chandler, *The Life and Work of John Mason Neale, 1818-1866* (Leominster: Gracewing, 1995).

page 74: On the Anglo-Catholic principle of sacramentality see Guillelmus Durandus, *The Symbolism of Churches and Church Ornaments*, trans. J.M. Neale and B. Webb (Leeds: T.W. Green, 1843; 3rd ed., London: Gibbings, 1906), xxvi-xxvii.

page 75: For the definition of papal infallibility at Vatican I, see *Decrees of the Ecumenical Councils*, ed. Norman P. Tanner, vol. 2, 815-16.

pages 75-76: John Henry Newman, *On Consulting the Faithful in Matters of Doctrine*, ed. John Coulson. Publisher (New York: Sheed & Ward, 1962); the quotation is on p. 77.

page 76: "The Syllabus of the Principal Errors of our times, which are stigmatized in the Consistorial Allocutions, Encyclicals and other Apostolic Letters of our Most Holy Father, Pope Pius IX," in C.A. Kertesz, ed., *Documents in the Political History of the European Continent* (Oxford: Clarendon, 1968), 233-44.

page 77: *The Fundamentals: A Testimony to the Truth, Compliments of Two Christian Laymen*, ed. A. C. Dixon, Louis Meyer, and R. A. Torrey (Chicago: Testimony, 1910-1915)

page 79: On Darby and his place in the millenarian traditions see Larry V. Crutchfield, *The Origins of Dispensationalism: The Darby Factor* (Lanham: University Press of America, 1992).

page 79: The "liver" pun appears in William James, *The Will to Believe, and Other Essays in Popular Philosophy*, ed. Frederick H. Burkhardt, Fredson Bowers, and Ignas K. Skrupskelis (Cambridge, Mass.: Harvard University Press, 1979), at the beginning of the second essay, "Is life worth living?", p34.

Page 80: The follower of Kant in question is Hans Vaihinger, author of *The Philosophy of 'As If': A System of the Theoretical, Practical and Religious Fictions of Mankind*, trans. C.K. Ogden (New York: Harcourt, Brace, 1925).

pages 82-83: On Schweitzer's interim ethics see J.I.H. McDonald, *Biblical Interpretation and Christian Ethics* (Cambridge: Cambridge University Press, 1993), 82-93.

pages 83-84: Rudolf Karl Bultmann, *New Testament and Mythology, and Other Basic Writings*, trans. Schubert M. Ogden (London: SCM, 1985). William A. Scott, *Historical Protestantism: An Historical Introduction to Protestant Theology* (Englewood Cliffs, N.J.: Prentice-Hall, 1970), gives concise and lucid accounts of his and other basic positions in Protestant Christianity.

pages 84-85: *Natural Theology: Comprising "Nature and Grace" by Professor Dr. Emil Brunner and the Reply "No!" by Dr. Karl Barth*, trans. Peter Fraenkel (London: Centenary, 1946; repr. Eugene, Oregon: Wipf & Stock, 2002).

page 86: Paul Tillich, *Dynamics of Faith* (New York: Harper, 1956).

page 86: Tillich's historical schema is in his *Interpretation of History*, trans. N. A. Rasetzki and Elsa L. Talmey (New York: Scribner, 1936).

page 87: Friedrich Nietzsche, *The Gay Science*, section 125, in *The Gay Science, with a Prelude in German Rhymes and an Appendix of Songs*, ed. Bernard Williams, trans. Josefine Nauckhoff and Adrian Del Caro (Cambridge: Cambridge University Press,

2001), 119-20. The theme occurs elsewhere in Nietzsche's works as well, but this is the *locus classicus*. The theme lies behind the old graffito that juxtaposes "God is dead! – Nietzsche" with "Nietzsche is dead! – God".

Acknowledgments

I am very much indebted to Barbara Newman for support, inspirations, and suggestions; to Alexander Lempke, also for support, and for help with the fine points; and to students who over the decades have borne up graciously with my representation of theology and its history.

BOOKS

O is a symbol of the world, of oneness and unity. In different cultures it also means the "eye," symbolizing knowledge and insight. We aim to publish books that are accessible, constructive and that challenge accepted opinion, both that of academia and the "moral majority."

Our books are available in all good English language bookstores worldwide. If you don't see the book on the shelves ask the bookstore to order it for you, quoting the ISBN number and title. Alternatively you can order online (all major online retail sites carry our titles) or contact the distributor in the relevant country, listed on the copyright page.

See our website www.o-books.net for a full list of over 500 titles, growing by 100 a year.

And tune in to myspiritradio.com for our book review radio show, hosted by June-Elleni Laine, where you can listen to the authors discussing their books.

MySpiritRadio